A New Yorker at Sea

NICK CATALANO

AEGEON PRESS, NEW YORK, N.Y.

Copyright © 2012 Nick Catalano
All rights reserved.

ISBN: 0615556965
ISBN 13: 9780615556963

Library of Congress Control Number: 2011918990
Aegeon Press New York N.Y.

Also by Nick Catalano

*Clifford Brown: The Life and
Art of the Legendary Jazz Trumpeter*

New York Nights

About The Author

Dr. Nick Catalano teaches music and literature at Pace University. He has sailed his sloop Segue in New York and East Hampton where he lives and writes. Each summer he cruises the Aegean.

Not that it matters, but virtually all of what follows is true and many of the incidents related continue to the present day. The narrative is set in the late 80's but since then pirates and terrorists have increased their activity, oil tanker spills have proliferated, and sail boats face greater collision threats from commercial ships.

N.C. 2012

1

I am a romantic. But the idea of sailing and the dream of adventure were always more appealing than the actual conditions at sea.

I fell in love with the beautiful lines of my sloop *Typee* and bought her instantly in 1981, but sailing her in any wind over twelve knots gave me the willies. Despite the strong wind gusts, I sailed in East Hampton's Gardiner's Bay time and again with friends and family—for the sheer romance.

I sailed from Three Mile Harbor to Shelter Island but sweated when I steered into the narrow channel at Coecles Harbor. I tried to hide my anxiety, but my abrupt language to my crews gave me away. Safely anchored, I sat in the cockpit eating, drinking, and sunning while I spoke authoritatively of the return of the ospreys and the history of the island. My guests, who referred to me as "Captain," seemed to enjoy my exaggerated storytelling, but they enjoyed the refreshments and swimming more than anything else. I gave the impression that I loved the challenge of wind and sea, but I was just as much of a city boy as my guests and avoided anything close to taking even the remotest of chances.

Still, I crewed in challenging races and signed on eagerly with friends for adventurous sailing charters in the Caribbean. I was partially motivated to do this because I had read widely of the adventures of others: the wild (and often apocryphal) stories of Tristan Jones, the authentic sagas of Sir Francis Chichester and *Gypsy Moth IV*, and the lonely circumnavigation log of Joshua Slocum. In books, sailing was always romantic and exciting.

I started racing in summer evening competitions in the local New York yacht clubs. These were light-winded, harmless short events a couple of hours long, followed by braggadocio imbibing at the yacht club bar.

One day, however, I was invited to crew aboard a boat entered in the Around Long Island Regatta—a race out in the Atlantic, around Montauk Point, and back to New York on Long Island Sound. I was a bit apprehensive about the ocean part, but the race would be held in late July when the seas were usually calm.

We started out in Staten Island on a Thursday afternoon, one of 192 boats in six competition classes. We headed out into the Atlantic with a stiff, fifteen-knot breeze in a weather front emanating from Hurricane Bob, which had dissipated in the Virginia Capes the night before. Spirits were high aboard my boat *Cassandra*—a thirty footer—despite the owner and his son vomiting all over the cockpit from seasickness right at the starting gun. As we soared out into the Atlantic, my romantic head was high, and I felt pretty safe because the navigator had chosen a course only a couple of

CHAPTER 1

miles south along the friendly Long Island beaches. Other boats tacked out farther into the ocean where, they calculated, the winds would be stronger.

The afternoon and evening were filled with happy shouting among the high-spirited crew, some swapping of the usually exaggerated racing stories, and occasional maneuvering of sails and sheets to get the best possible speed. I was at the helm, imagining myself to be Ted Turner captaining an America's Cup race. My major skill was steering, so I avoided manning winches and hauling sheets lest my crewmates discover my on-deck ineptitude.

Actually, they were impressed with my steady course maintenance and my steadfast refusal to be relieved at the helm. So, I continued straight and true, constantly reassured at the sight of the Long Island beaches only a mile or two on my port side.

I stayed at the helm late into darkness and was reluctant to go below for some shut-eye because of the seasickness. I wanted to snack, but as soon as I encountered the horrible smell down below, I changed my mind.

I lay in the windward bunk. The boat was heeling, so I had to wedge myself hard onto the bunk else I would be thrown to the floor. I ceded the leeward bunk to my seasick crewmates so they could rest easier. But after an hour of tossing and wedging my body on the impossible slant of my bunk, I gave up trying to sleep. I simply shut my eyes and kept trying to stop myself from falling out onto the floor. As the time passed, I slowly began to sense that the boat was climbing deeper and deeper swells.

After a half hour of this wild motion, during which time the mast began to make louder and louder banging sounds,

I sat up. "What the hell is going on?" I asked no one in particular. The hatch boards to the cockpit were up, so I could neither see nor hear what was happening up top. Rather than alert the crew in a frightened voice, I reached for the VHF radio and turned to the weather channel.

I caught the forecaster in mid-sentence: "And so Hurricane Bob has partially reformed itself, picked up speed and intensity, and is now about twenty miles south of Montauk Point headed northeast....It'll present real danger to the Around Long Island racing fleet." Static interrupted the forecast.

"Holy shit," I said to myself as I dropped to the floor donning my foul weather gear, shoes, and safety harness.

I hid my fear as I removed the hatch boards and ascended the steps to the cockpit. "Gettin' a little rough up here," I said, trying to muster some bravado. But when I reached the top step, my heartbeat went wild. Walls of water rose in every direction, and the roar of the ocean drowned out our voices. The wind speed indicator read sixty-five knots, and the needle was moving steadily upward. The mast was banging so fiercely I was sure it would rip right out of the hull.

"Oh, dear God," I said. "So this is what it's like sailing in a hurricane." The cockpit crew had expressions of horror on their faces. In a panic I shouted, "I'll take the helm if you'd like a blow—"

Pete Drollinger, an experienced racing helmsman, let the wheel go instantly and dived for the steps to the cabin.

I staggered to the helm and, with clumsy fingers, clipped my harness to the rail. I struggled to sit erect and look calm as I fought with the wheel.

CHAPTER 1

The hurricane howl of the wind was frightening. I glanced at the anemometer, which was now at seventy-five knots but, unlike before, now seemed steady. The wind was now blowing so hard that it was shearing off the tops of waves. The water all around us was boiling white foam.

From the cabin steps, Pete shouted up to us. He had been listening to the VHF weather broadcast. "The coast guard is going nuts," he said. "There are dismastings of racers all over the place. At least six boats have overturned but, so far, no confirmed casualties."

After ten minutes or so, I silently took stock. We were at Montauk and by the shape of the land we had probably passed the lighthouse, but I couldn't be sure. The compass had me heading northwest, and the wind was directly on my stern, heaving *Cassandra* forward and forcing her to surf so violently that I thought we would pitchpole any second. The only piece of sail we had up was a handkerchief jib for steerage.

We were literally flying through the water but, thankfully, in the right direction. I thought, after awhile, that the mast didn't seem to be banging so loud. As I tried to maintain the semblance of a course, I stole a look at the anemometer: sixty knots and dropping.

In under an hour we had roared by Plum Island and were well into Long Island Sound. I spun the wheel harder to port and headed westward finding I could keep her steady at 275 degrees. I hadn't noticed, but all the crew were now next to me in the cockpit, laughing and joking. "Can I have a beer?" someone asked.

I was about to throw him a hard look but the anemometer, which read forty knots, caught my attention. Incredible, I thought. This crazy storm is passing us.

"Hey, I wonder if we've moved ahead of the other boats. I can't see even one anywhere," said Pete.

Wow. Could we actually be in front? The idea grabbed me hard. Gritting my teeth, I shouted, "Loosen the starboard jib sheet and give us more speed." The crew sprang to my order. I smiled to myself and basked in my triumph. But it was short-lived. You've really gone loony, I thought. After being scared shitless, suddenly some crazy confidence has buried your fear. It was uncanny. Sailing in forty knots of wind should have terrified me, but there I was, urging the boat onward with the madness of a modern-day Ahab.

And because faster boats in our class with far more skillful sailors were dismasted or otherwise crippled, we sailed across the finish line in first place. Go figure.

✯ ✯ ✯

For the Caribbean charters, I had a few friends who knew about as much as I did but, in some cases, had more experience. I took great comfort in numbers and felt we could probably handle anything thrown at us and would always be close to land. My friends were classic New York businessmen, and their competitiveness extended into their leisure pursuits. That spirit of macho aggression, which permeated the group, actually hid much individual insecurity.

CHAPTER 1

We sailed the Drake Channel in the Virgin Islands and the Grenadines a few times. I was always excited at the prospect—beautiful islands, lovely harbors, and gorgeous sunsets. But even though I read a lot, I couldn't master knot-tying, got very nervous at docking, and was always fearful of anyone discovering that I wasn't as confident as I appeared to be.

One night, we anchored in a quiet cove of Mayreau Island in the Grenadines. It was an idyllic setting; we saw only two other boats. For me, the magic of the scene resembled what you'd find in a glossy travel magazine. There we were, joyously drinking and telling tall tales, eagerly anticipating a sumptuous dinner that we ourselves had prepared: grilled mahi mahi, mushroom salad, and local melons. We had sailed from St. Vincent to Bequia and, after struggling with raising the main in the huge swells—a feat that rattled our nerves—we cruised along nicely and arrived safely.

I smiled, then, as I recalled how panicky the conversation was in tight spots and, conversely, how full of bravado we all were when we were in control.

After the inevitably brilliant sunset and dinner (always more appetizing at sea), we laughed and story-told late into the night when, suddenly, a silent wave came crashing into us beam on. And before we could register what had just happened, we were hit with another, and then another. Dinner plates shattered as they hit the floor, our drinks were knocked over.

We scurried for flashlights, which, when turned on, revealed scared looks on our faces. After a few anxious moments, we realized that the waves were rollers coming to haunt us in the dark from way out in the ocean.

We grabbed our guide books, consulted with one of the other boats in the cove, and discovered that we had to quickly re-adjust our anchorage—or we would be ignominiously thrown onto the beach to face huge embarrassment and expense from our charter company. Fearfully, but with extreme care, we managed a Bahamian moor anchoring, which took us two hours amid confusion and a few impolite exchanges: "I told you to let the line go. What the fuck's the matter with you?" and "Aw, go fuck yourself. Next time you do it."

Later, as the crisis ebbed and more drinking s-l-o-w-l-y restored camaraderie, we retired to our bunks. But my anxiety lingered. It was the first of many restless nights.

One of the most popular chartering areas in the Caribbean is the American- British Virgin Island group. The islands surround the Sir Francis Drake Channel, a calm body of water where bareboat charterers such as we were could sail in relative safety and enjoy the warm sun of the southern islands.

My crewmates wanted to get away from their wives, party away their time, and get suntans to impress their secretaries. They made mental notes of those incidents during the sail that they could embellish on at cocktail parties and office water-fountain gatherings. We always chartered in January because I wasn't in session at my university, the prevailing easterlies were steady, and the weather was clear.

Virgin Island sailing has come to resemble a visit to a theme park. On Monday night, there is a pig roast on Jost Van Dyke. Tuesdays are reserved for free scuba classes on Virgin Gorda. On Wednesdays, yachties have dining privileges on upscale Peter Island. And on Fridays, snorkeling lessons are offered at St. John's. If you charter there more than once, the sailing experience quickly turns into the

CHAPTER 1

usual picture taking, sunbathing, drinking, and dining ritual of an ordinary island holiday vacation.

Despite the ease, we still managed some hairy moments. On Mondays, the idea was to anchor early at Jost Van Dyke for a good spot close to the beach, where we could easily dinghy over and get good seats at the pig roast. We found a nice location, but it was very close to other boats. We maneuvered carefully, maintaining the yachting protocol of total calmness. All eyes were watching as we weighed anchor. But our demeanor wasn't up to snuff. "Let out the slack or we'll be too close!" was enough to elicit a smirk from a neighboring sailor sipping his piña colada. "Just relax boys," he said. "You'll get it right one of these days."

Having to listen to such sass from yachties was always a pain.

In addition to the physical challenges of sailing, there's the stress of making sure you operate according to Hoyle, or some wise ass will always be ready to criticize so he can score points with his guests and aggrandize his macho personality.

2

My fantasies increased as my reading of sailing sagas began to focus on circumnavigations. The most compelling tale involved a unique French sailor named Bernard Moitessier. He had undertaken several challenges in his life, which sailing magazines had recorded, but he really immortalized himself in the Golden Globe Race of 1968–69. The event, sponsored by the *Sunday Times* of London, was formidable: a solo circumnavigation without stops. There were nine entrants who could start any time they chose within a window of a few months. The sailors were all luminaries and included Chay Blyth, who had actually rowed across the Atlantic; Robin Knox-Johnston, a racing legend; and Moitessier.

The race was predictably grueling with several entrants dropping out in the first leg, from England down to the Cape of Good Hope. One sailor—Donald Crowhurst—actually tried to radio false positions to gain advantage. John

Ridgway succumbed to loneliness and Nigel Tetley eventually sank.

But the amazing story was about Moitessier aboard *Joshua*. After almost completing the race and in a position to win, he did an extraordinary thing: he decided that racing competitions violated the spirit and history of sailing, so he changed his course. He veered away from the finish line and kept sailing.

Instead of coming home as the conquering hero and claiming prize money, trophies, and fame, he continued sailing alone and almost completed a second solo circumnavigation. He said, "People who do not know that a sailboat is a living creature will never understand anything about boats and the sea."

I have always spun this quote as either a reflection of Moitessier's deep poetic awareness of the sea or his encroaching dementia from being out there too long.

Other stories of circumnavigations piqued my interest. Eric and Susan Hiscock, for example, made several circumnavigations, some when they were quite old. Robin Knox-Johnston became the fastest solo circumnavigator in 1969, and Tania Aebi would become the youngest female solo circumnavigator aboard her Contessa 26 *Varuna*.

The idea of circumnavigation became a symbol of the supreme romantic achievement—an equivalency of medieval knighthood. But, during the 1980s, the sheer number of people accomplishing this feat in various contexts was becoming quite large, with the result that the romance associated with it was steadily diminishing.

Then, one day, my imaginative excitement returned suddenly. In a series of long-distance phone calls from the

CHAPTER 2

Caroline Islands near the Philippines, I spoke to the captain of *Bravura*, a fifty-one-foot cutter that had been circumnavigating for two years. A crew member had to leave after the boat finished beating up the Red Sea, and I agreed to replace him and sail onward.

I couldn't believe it. The captain had read a piece I had written about the Around Long Island race in 1985 and decided to contact me. Predictably all sorts of imaginative thoughts entered my head. I had taught Homer's *Odyssey* for years and, now, I was about to sail in the Mediterranean and his "wine- dark" sea. I envisioned exotic locations and mysterious cultures and people I would encounter in that part of the world.

But somehow, the perils of sailing and the stress and fears that I had experienced during my blue water charters and other sails couldn't displace my romantic dreams.

I was expected to meet *Bravura* in Egypt, where terrorism seemed to be happening almost every day, from hijackings to hostage kidnapping—all accomplished with violent, mind-numbing acts. Who could forget what happened to Leon Klinghoffer when he and his wheelchair were tossed over from the Italian cruise ship *Achille Lauro*? I had to brush aside these thoughts if I wanted to undertake this particular voyage.

I had arranged to get to Egypt through Athens, visit with some travel associates who organized the travel seminar that I taught each year in Greece, and fly on to Cairo. In Athens, my friends were eager to hear about my upcoming voyage. Late night dinner parties were filled with my usual sailing stories and speculations on joining the circumnavigation of *Bravura*. My friends were eager for information, and I was quite content playing the role of a modern-day Columbus, calmly describing the life adventures of a major league sailor.

I flew to Cairo and spent hours waiting to pass through immigration and customs. The airport was gloomy, and the Egyptian personnel reminded me of characters from an eerie '40s film noir.

At last I reached the customs booth. The customs officer took his time reviewing my passport, visa, and travel documents, slowly turning pages and cross-checking data. Finally, I said none too politely, "Is there anything wrong?" I checked my watch and fidgeted for effect. He ignored my question and, when he was good and ready, he raised his head from the paperwork and said, "Do not be impatient. You are in the Middle East now."

His words stuck in my craw as I hailed a taxi and rode through streets where beggars and hustlers pushed and shoved their way among dilapidated pushcarts. The crowds were ominously thick, and the cab driver occasionally commented on the seamy sights. "There have been several bombings of late" was the remark that truly punctuated this disheartening entry into Egypt.

So much for the glories of Ramses and the ancient Egyptian sphinx, which had consumed my thoughts ever since I knew I'd be going to Cairo. I sat in the cab for the rest of the traffic-stalled ride, with sinking feelings.

I arrived at the Ramses Hilton, a hotel I never would have chosen except that my travel associates in Athens had gotten me a very low rate. I had secret little hatreds for monster chain hotels; still, the Ramses location on the Nile had sounded tempting. At the check-in desk, the clerk told me

CHAPTER 2

there had been a small hitch in my reservation. He looked at me slyly. "I can change your room with another that has a splendid Nile view," he said.

I stammered a bit and hesitated. Then I blurted, "Well, of course, that would be great." In my confusion, the thought occurred to me that he might ask for something in return. I looked at him, and his expression definitely suggested that money should be coming to him forthwith. I thought for a moment as I gathered my wallet and reached for my bags.

I'm not reading him right, I thought. I've seen a lot of hustling in my day, but I've never had a reservation clerk ask me for a bribe.

My room was spacious and comfortable, and my mood elevated. Then, I opened the curtains wide and frowned. My "Nile view" was a fog-encased embankment lined with more of those pathetic pushcarts.

To lighten my mood, I decided to treat myself to an elaborate dinner and, as I ordered a drink at the dining room bar, a well-dressed guy with a ruddy face turned to me. "Well, yank, how do you like the Nile view?"

He was with his wife and daughter, and it looked like they had been shopping. His accent sounded Australian.

"Well, it isn't exactly what I expected," I replied.

He told me he was a New Zealander and, when I told him I was joining a circumnavigation, he launched into a loud diatribe on how the Kiwis were going to clobber the United States in the upcoming running of the America's Cup. I chose to be polite instead of telling him that he was crazy. Still, we traded talk reflecting our considerable knowledge of this famous race and laughed as we toasted the entrants. But his insistence on how the Americans were going to get their ears pinned back was almost rude. I smiled as the hostess called me to my table and wished him and the Kiwi racers good luck as I sat down to dine.

After another drink and some pork terrine, Nile perch, and creamy yogurt, I went to my room feeling exhilarated by what lay ahead. Tomorrow I'll visit the pyramids was my last thought before sleep came on.

Of course I had read up on the ancient pyramid of Cheops outside of Cairo. Built about 2,500 BCE and the only one of the Seven Wonders of the World left standing, this ancient tomb is easily the most spectacular attraction of any Cairo visit.

As I taxied through the desert, my thoughts went back to the ancient pharaohs, the mysterious hieroglyphics, and the stories of the longest-lasting empire in world history. Shelley's sonnet "Ozymandias," with its ironical tale of Ramses II, who reigned 1279–1213 BC, had always fascinated me. Ramses' construction of the temples at Abu Simbel, his consort Nefertari, his association with Moses, and his monumental ego were the stuff of legends.

The wondrous, imaginative constructs in my head began to crumble, even before we arrived at the site, because my cab driver had initiated an unending caterwaul, trying to sell me souvenir wares that occupied the entire front of the cab. He had plastic pyramid models, horrific statues of sphinxes, tapes of "original" ancient Egyptian music, imitation fez headwear, canned dates from the "oldest" palm trees in existence, and other cheap artifacts. Even after I declined his offers half a dozen times, he kept ranting. His selling technique involved laughing and joking, followed by pleas of poverty and then threatening commentary. "Unless

CHAPTER 2

you make some purchases," he said, "the cab fare will cost double."

Exasperated, I finally answered his cacophony with louder refusals of my own which, only after making me hoarse, finally shut him up. By this time we had arrived at the great pyramid. I shoved open the door and threw the fare at him, which included a tip he certainly didn't deserve. But he wasn't finished. As I slung my travel bag over my shoulder and began my trek to the site, he ran after me shouting what sounded like curses. He was uncontrollable. I finally stopped and turned in my tracks and screamed back at him as loud as I could, waving my arms hysterically. He stopped dead, changed the expression on his face to one of resignation, rubbed his beard, jauntily walked back to the cab, and sped off.

I was livid. I tried to gather my thoughts and, as I looked up at the pyramid, retrieve my reminiscences of Ramses. After walking about fifty yards or so, I had half succeeded in this when I was accosted by several other hawkers selling the same cheap souvenirs as the cab driver. I drove them off with my ready retorts, only to run into an eager lad who practically ran over me with his camel. He insisted that a ride on the beast was the only important event at the site.

"Sirrah, sirrah, only five hundred piastres and you will have the time of your life. He is easy to ride and he won't bite."

I hadn't even raised my hands in refusal when he took my picture next to the camel and started a sales pitch for the photo.

If my description of these hustlers sounds a bit harsh, it should be remembered that I had had years of experience in Turkey, South America, and Africa dealing with some similarly uncompromising characters. Any tourist should certainly expect this and, after dozens of encounters, I had actually come to enjoy some of the bargaining; I'd even instructed my students on the protocol. All of this resulted in some nice bargains and also the satisfaction that I was contributing in a small way to the welfare of some pretty poor people.

But these Egyptian clowns were something else.

After the camel episode, I walked on toward the Great Pyramid of Giza and tried to distract myself with thoughts of the ancient Egyptians and their construction methods. I had always felt that the awesome reverence paid to this tomb by millions of people for thousands of years was mostly because of its size. Yes, it was one of the Seven Wonders, but it was a very fundamental geometric shape; and it was built with armies of either slave labor or tax debtors, depending on which theory you believed.

I had spent years lecturing on the Parthenon in Athens, which was a much more significant architectural triumph. Its purposeful curves to correct the distortion of the human eye, its masterful sculpture, and its humanistic theme made it much more important than the structure before me.

I reflected on the ancient Egyptian beliefs. They were so committed to the notion of life after death that their dentists made sure to fill cavities of the corpses so they could chew properly in the afterlife. I recalled that the only Egyptian pharaoh to reject the traditional belief system was Akhenaten, who ruled in the Eighteenth Dynasty for about seventeen years. He dared to challenge the ancient priesthood, but they had the last word. When he died, in about

CHAPTER 2

1,336 BCE, the priests erased all records of his reign because they were terrified that the religious power they had over the people would be challenged. So much for the attempt to think for oneself in ancient Egypt.

I made my way to the admission booth for the Great Pyramid. It was a dark, cloudy April day, so there were only a few people about. Still in the throes of my reverie of Akhenaten, I initially didn't hear the ticket taker when he said something about "the special private tour."

I suddenly snapped to and, after looking at him hard, realized that I was being hustled yet again.

Disgusted, I paid my piastres, proceeded to the entrance of the pyramid, and prepared to crawl into the small opening.

I made my way inside and, after struggling a bit with the lengthy crawl, found myself in a small, empty chamber. The guide books had referenced the space saying it wasn't very important. After I gazed around, I decided the guide book was right so I crawled back out and prepared myself for the big hustle once again.

I got away from the hustlers and, a little bit off in the distance, took some photos. I've never been eager to photograph places I've been, and I often wonder why I even bring a camera. But, I succumbed to the tourists' disease and half-heartedly snapped away.

As I left the site, I grew annoyed realizing that my biggest memory during my visit to the Great Pyramid of Cheops would be of the Egyptians who tried to hustle me.

After another day in Cairo, during which time I had acquired some papyri in order to help with some research I was planning to do on the ancient library in Alexandria, I bargained my way through the shops and made other small purchases for the upcoming voyage on *Bravura*.

I made arrangements for a car to take me across the hundred-mile stretch of desert to Port Suez, where, hopefully, *Bravura* had arrived. The hotel clerk told me that he would get a driver for a reasonable rate. Naturally, I would have to pay the clerk a commission.

My car turned out to be a battered jeep, and my driver, Abdul, was a cheerful sort who proudly showed me his collection of audio tapes. I made sure to review the agreed-upon price, and we were off once again through the crowded streets and hopeless traffic of downtown Cairo.

Initially, Abdul kept up an unsolicited banter, complaining about the politics of Anwar Sadat and the endless problems of overpopulation in Cairo. As we reached the desert, he started to show off his knowledge of western music and American culture, rattling off the names of performers and gossiping about celebrities who were having affairs.

As we got further away from the city, the heat of the desert intensified. Even though it was only April, the temperature soared. Soon, I saw a grim visage of debris left over from the Yom Kippur War of 1973 strewn everywhere. There were abandoned tanks and trucks, pillboxes, and rusting artillery pieces all over. It had been fifteen years since the fighting had stopped, but it seemed as though it was yesterday that hostilities ended because absolutely no effort had been made to clean up anything. I asked Abdul about this, but he shrugged his shoulders saying that this desert garbage was by far the least of Egypt's problems.

Thirty miles into our journey, perspiration was stinging my eyes, making it difficult to see the stretch of what appeared to be undulating desert through a rolling wall of heat. I pulled a bottle of water from my bag and swilled heartily before offering some to Abdul. He shook his head and, when I tried to press the bottle in his hand, he lurched away from it and said, "Ramadan."

I nodded, impressed with his piety. I quickly slipped the bottle back into my bag, feeling like an infidel.

As we approached the war-torn outskirts of Suez, Abdul described the extreme poverty and dire state of his family and friends. Existence was a day-to-day affair in the country and, as I gazed at the scantily clad children and the garbage-riddled streets of the town we were passing, I told him how sorry I was for him and hoped things would get better.

We pulled into a run-down depot that Abdul indicated was the center of town. From here, he said, I could easily make my way down to the harbor. I thanked him, shook his hand, and gave him his money.

He looked at the wad of piastres. "But this is no good, my friend. This is not enough," he said.

I was incredulous. "What do you mean? We went over the cost twice back in Cairo."

He started yelling "No good, no good. My cab is broken and I have to pay money! The gasoline is too expensive…" He rattled on and on in frustration. "You are cheating me! You are cheating me!" he roared.

He was so angry that, for a second, he had me believing that I really was cheating him. Quickly, I collected my thoughts. "Look, Abdul," I said. "We agreed on a price and that is that. I'm not going to listen to your arguments and accusations." I picked up my bags and walked away.

"You Americans are evil. You are trying to destroy my country!"

The passersby looked over at us. I was about to lose my cool and scream back but, when I looked back at Abdul, he was calmly adjusting his radio as he turned the car around. The obligatory hustle was obviously over for him and, when he saw that he could achieve nothing more, he instantly relented. And that, ladies and gentlemen, was that.

I shook my head as I walked down the street. How long would it take me to get used to the madness of the Middle East?

3

The streets of Suez reminded me of the bombed-out ruins of Berlin at the end of World War II that I had seen in films. Everywhere there was desolation. There were some half-empty stalls where the meat was insect-ridden and the fruit was rotten. The people were in tatters and slowly walked about with expressions of hopelessness. Although I was obviously a weird sight with my strange clothing and baggage, they barely noticed me.

I made my way down toward the water and felt like an idiot asking a teenaged boy, "Do you know where the Port Suez Yacht Club is?" He shook his head gloomily but pointed toward the water. After I stopped to inquire twice more, I finally arrived at a high stone wall in faded pink with a guard booth. I cautiously walked through the entrance, expecting to be abruptly halted. But the guard, if there was one, was not around. I took the path that turned downward toward the water.

Back in Cairo, I had worried that *Bravura* wouldn't make it on schedule. Where the hell am I going to go in this godforsaken place if my boat isn't here? My mind was racing, and my fear increased as a couple of armed soldiers approached. But, after looking me up and down, they passed and, as I walked toward the basin, I finally saw some pleasure boats.

Near the water I was able to view the expanse of the Port Suez Yacht Club. As I surveyed the area, I chuckled to myself; "yacht club" didn't exactly describe the facility in front of me. What I saw was eight pleasure boats in various states of low maintenance with bowlines all attached to a large, battered, anchored buoy. The buoy was in the center of a small inlet the size of a football field adjacent to the Suez Canal. And, as I took in the scene, the bow of a huge oil tanker plunged into view. As soon as the Leviathan sped by, the entire vista was blocked out by the sweep of the biggest vessel I had ever seen.

The specter of this scene immediately sank whatever expectations I might have had of anticipation and adventure. The filth and garbage that filled the shoreline was fittingly accompanied by black smoke from the tanker and the smell of oil everywhere. A gloomier sight, I could not imagine.

As I focused on the pleasure boats tied up to the buoy, I suddenly realized that the sleek lines of a large sailboat had been hidden by the other crafts. I moved down the shore quickly and soon caught the name *Bravura* on the starboard bow.

So this was it. My pulse accelerated at the thought that I had made it. I had traveled thousands of miles, crossed a

CHAPTER 3

war-torn desert, and had fortuitously caught up with her at last.

I almost called out "Ahoy!" but quickly realized that I was too far away. When I saw that there was no dinghy service, I stopped. I saw a small rowboat and, ignoring the possibility that it might belong to somebody, threw my bags in and shoved off. If I had taken somebody's craft, then I would deal with the problem later. I anxiously rowed to *Bravura* and rehearsed my introductory greetings.

As I neared the swim ladder on her stern, I noticed that her once-white freeboard was now faded and stained. She looked tired, and I saw that there were small piles of sand on her deck. Beating up the Red Sea had certainly taken a toll.

"Ahoy, *Bravura*, anybody home?" I yelled loudly and then waited. A dirty, sweaty body came out of the cabin. A graybeard wearing grimy, rimless glasses looked down at me suspiciously. "Who're you?" he asked in a raspy voice.

I gave him my best smile. "Oh, I'm Joe Pisano. I'm the replacement crew." I stood up proudly in the rowboat.

"I guess you're the guy from New York," he said, not impressed. "I'm Roger Thornton." He looked around. "Dick Spooner is around somewhere." He scratched his back with a wrench he was holding. Then he made a hook with his other arm and motioned for me to grab it. "C'mon aboard…. The boat is a real mess, and we're tryin' to repair the engine." Then he turned and left me standing there alone.

Well, that was a royal welcome, I thought, as I struggled to get my bags onto *Bravura*'s stern from my unsteady rowboat.

Indeed the boat was a mess. Inside the cabin I quickly surveyed the situation: piles of dirty dishes around the sink, rumpled laundry on the settee, nautical charts strewn among rulers on the navigation table, and empty cans of food rolling around the floor.

A pair of black hands gripped the companionway, and a black face appeared among an opening in the food cans. Up sprung a body supported by the hands.

"How do" said the black face. As the tall, portly man straightened up, I saw that the blackness was dark grease and oil from the engine compartment down under the rolling cans. "I'm Dick Spooner." He extended his hand to shake mine but, realizing that it was filthy, withdrew it. He smiled. "I'm working on the engine."

"How's it going?" I asked him, summoning my best tone of support. He looked down at the floor hatchway and shook his head. "Not good…not good…there's diesel fuel in the oil pan. It looks like the fuel injectors are worn out." He looked back up at me; on his black face was a look of defeat. "We had to run the engine a lot up the Red Sea 'cause there was a thirty-knot wind right in our faces for most of the twelve hundred miles."

"Couldn't you tack and sail at all?" I asked.

He looked at me hard. "We kept tryin', but if we got too close to shore there were always guys with rifles that kept shootin' at us. So much for an American flag on our transom."

I shivered at this disheartening news but forced a smile. "Anything I can do to help?" I instantly recognized that life had not been going too well for the crew of *Bravura*, and if I wanted their acceptance, I would have to hit the deck running.

"Oh, yeah," he said quickly. "Most of our food has rotted 'cause something's wrong with the reefer. Guess you can get started with that."

CHAPTER 3

I was about to ask what the "reefer" was, but Dick hopped down below the floorboards and back into the engine compartment.

I grabbed my bags and threw them into a pile in a small corner of the galley. I was determined to prove that I wouldn't be a useless passenger.

As I looked around, I simultaneously eyed and smelled some potatoes that were on the shelf of the open refrigerator door. The odor intensified as I got closer. When I opened the door, I saw melted butter and opened containers of warm milk lying next to rotting cheese and fruit.

I rolled up my sleeves and started taking out all the bad food. "Don't throw that food away," said Roger abruptly as he entered the galley. We're really low on supplies, and that may have to be our supper tonight." Carrying an armful of tools, he headed for the navigation table. "Gotta re-adjust the sat-nav," he said.

I got the feeling that he was wondering why I wasn't working as frantically as he and Dick were.

"What seems to be wrong with the reefer?" I asked. I had picked up a screwdriver and was trying to open the back panel. In fact, I knew nothing about refrigerators and was not exactly Mr. Fixit.

"Don't know," said Roger above the din of an electric motor. It's got plenty of Freon."

I spent the next hour tinkering with parts of the reefer. I realized I hadn't the foggiest idea what I was doing, and was obviously way out of my league in this company of sailing superstars. I panicked. What would they say when they discovered I was all thumbs mechanically? What would happen when I screwed up royally in some tricky sailing maneuver?

Why did I recoil so horrifically when I saw the sloppy mess in the galley? These guys had come halfway around the world and were calmly repairing their vessel while I was having a landlubber anxiety attack.

I knew that Dick and his wife had circumnavigated before from the telephone briefing I had received from the Carolines. Roger and his girlfriend were *Bravura*'s owners and had sailed oceans extensively. They seemed like okay guys, but they weren't exactly overfriendly. I don't know what I was expecting—big smiles of welcome and a vodka tonic, perhaps? Instead, I got a messy kitchen with flies swarming rotten food and a crippled engine.

I kept "working" at the reefer for another hour, making sure that the guys could see that I was determined when they walked to and fro attending to their own tasks.

The setting rays of the sun hit me in the eyes after awhile, and I felt that maybe it was okay to stop working and go out on deck. Roger and Dick had been up there for some time working on the rigging. I went up and put an angry look on my face. "Goddamn, if I can find out what's wrong with that reefer," I said as I spit into the sea and sat down in the cockpit. Roger and Dick looked over but said nothing. But I knew what they were thinking.

They continued discussing the engine problem. "I can't do much about those injectors, Roger," Dick was saying. "I looked in the manual, and there's an International Diesel dealer with a repair service listed in Cairo."

Roger looked out over the water. "It'll probably cost a fortune getting a mechanic over here from Cairo."

"Well, Rog, I'm tellin' you, I can't do anything. I can't machine new injector rods for chrissake."

CHAPTER 3

I couldn't understand why Dick sounded so defensive. It surprised me that he had even thought about doing something like that.

"I didn't realize you fellas had machine tools aboard. That's pretty amazing," I interjected, trying to calm things down.

Roger looked at me sharply. "You'd be a fool to try circumnavigating without that capability," he said.

"I've already machined a new prop shaft," said Dick, joining Roger in the lecture.

"Gee, that's terrific," I said lamely.

"Well, somebody's gonna have to go to Cairo to get a repair guy," said Roger.

Silence followed, but all eyes were on me. I dreaded the idea of going back through that miserable desert and then having to haggle with more Egyptians.

"Isn't there some way to telephone the company?" I asked.

Dick smirked. "I can't imagine tryin' to find a phone back there in that mess," he said, nodding toward the bombed-out ruins of Port Suez.

I stood up. "Well, I think I'd like to try," I said. I felt confident for the first time since coming aboard.

The guys were shaking their heads. "Okay," said Roger. "See if you can get us some beer while you're scrounging around." He got up and went down into the cabin.

I wasn't happy, but it got my dander up a little. Dammit, I thought. There's gotta be at least one phone in that town.

After I got the International Diesel phone number and pertinent information from Dick, I gathered my gear, strutted to the stern, and climbed down into the rowboat.

By the time I got to shore, most of my determination had evaporated. Where the hell would I find a phone? I hadn't seen any stores on my way down to the water, and no one looked friendly or approachable.

I walked down some alleys into smaller streets. I passed two groups of kids, one just sitting around and the other playing some game with a stuffed rag. All of the kids were in faded, tattered clothes. They looked at me oddly, but I decided to try a question.

"Does anybody know where I can find a telephone?"

The game-playing group stopped, and then both groups wandered over and gathered around. I repeated the question, but they just looked at one another and then back at me. A couple shrugged their shoulders. It quickly became obvious that no one spoke English.

I started to move along, but the group closed in on me without hostility. One kid put his hand out with a begging motion, and soon they all followed suit.

Oh boy. Here we go.

I kept walking but reached into my pocket, turned around, and threw some coins in their direction. The kids cheered loudly, and I felt a swift pang of sympathy. I threw a few more coins at the group and then walked away, trying to focus on my task.

I stopped twice again in my meanderings through the ruins of Port Suez. I was again met with confusion; the first was a middle-aged guy pulling boxes through an alley entrance and the other a young woman wearing a burka. She put her hand up to her face when she realized I was a foreigner, so I backed off quickly.

The sun had set, and the streets were getting dark quickly. So was my mood. I was running out of people to ask and ideas to explore. I looked up at the only street light in the area and saw a wire leading from the pole to the best looking house on the street.

I couldn't believe it, but I found myself knocking on the front door after I saw people inside through a lit window. Immediately, the latches clicked and the door sprang open. Standing there was a tall man with a huge black beard and dark, penetrating eyes. Behind him stood a tiny woman, presumably his wife, holding a child in one arm and the hand of a young boy next to her.

All I could think of was how alarmed I would be if I saw a foreigner standing at my door in the darkness.

Without thinking, I started to speak rapidly. "Excuse me, sir, but I am desperately looking for a telephone to make an emergency phone call." I was hoping that he understood some English.

"Who are you?" he asked, his eyes flashing.

"I—I'm an American from one of the boats down in the yacht club. We're in trouble and need to phone for help." I put as much desperation into my voice as possible, in part to disguise the spark of joy and relief I felt when I heard him speak English.

He softened a bit, but the fear on his wife's face remained. "Do you have a telephone I could use? I would be very grateful and would pay you to use it," I continued, summoning more urgency.

He looked back inside the house at his family, then down at the floor, then up at me. "Come inside," he said, still looking serious.

I wanted to hug him but held out my hand instead and half-cried, "Thank you so much." I stepped into the first

Islamic kitchen I had ever seen in my life and waited for his instructions. He took my arm and ushered me deeper into a small, very modest apartment. We were in a hallway and there, by god, on the wall was a telephone.

"Where do you want to call?" he asked. I was ecstatic and fumbled for the paper with the numbers on it.

"It's in Cairo," I said. "I'm trying to contact the International Diesel office. Our engine is leaking oil, and we need a mechanic to come out and repair it."

He calmly took the paper, dialed the number, and spoke to someone in Arabic. He turned to me. "What is the name of your boat?" he asked.

"*Bravura*. It's on a circumnavigation and has just come up the Red Sea."

After conversing some more, he turned and said to me, "You will have to pay for the transportation of the mechanic."

"Yes, yes, of course," I said, tingling with anticipation.

He spoke again at length and then hung up. "They will send someone tomorrow afternoon. They know where the yacht club is."

I couldn't resist. I took him by the hand and put my other hand on his shoulder. "I don't know how to thank you, sir. Please, please accept my gratitude. May I pay you for the use of your phone?"

"No, that will not be necessary," he said quietly. He extended his arm toward the door and said, "And now I have work to do." Uncertain, I moved to the door still uttering "thank you," still wanting to shower this poor family with all the money I was carrying.

I turned at the doorway and looked at them. The expression of alarm and concern hadn't left any of their faces. Although

CHAPTER 3

he'd helped me more than he could imagine, he wanted me out. I thanked him for the twentieth time and, before he closed the door, I asked, "Sir, is there a store nearby where I can buy some food?" He quickly uttered something about a light on the next street and then abruptly closed the door.

Well, it wasn't classic hospitality, but he sure saved my ass.

Emboldened now, I strutted in the direction he indicated and, sure enough, there appeared a large pushcart with someone standing beside it. As I got closer, I saw that the pushcart was empty. I approached the dark figure standing next to it. "I need to buy some beer," I said.

The hunched man stood upright quickly, and a cynical, smiling expression formed on his face. He obviously understood English. I was starting to feel lucky.

"Where are you from?" he asked as he moved toward the pushcart.

"I'm an American. I'm on a boat down at the basin." I pointed at the harbor.

"Don't you know that it is the holy time of Ramadan?" He said this admonishingly. "We are not allowed to have liquor or food during the sacred time."

I was humbled instantly. "I—I'm sorry…yes, I know that it is the time of Ramadan. I suppose I should have been more respectful. I was only trying to help out my crewmates…" I lowered my head not finishing the sentence. I wanted to apologize more forcefully, but I didn't know how.

"I am Mahommet. Come with me." It was an order. Meekly, I followed in his footsteps. I didn't know where we were going, but I felt that I had insulted him and whatever he wanted me to do, I had to comply.

We wound through the bombed-out streets and alleys in a maze of turns and climbs. We walked for at least ten minutes in total darkness, and I started worrying about how I would get back to the boat.

We came to a tall, barn-like structure situated in a cul-de-sac. I could barely make out the doors in the dark but soon realized that they were massive. Mahommet took out a ring of keys. He selected a large one and then took out a pencil flashlight and shone it on the door. It turned out that there were several large padlocks. He took his time with each of them.

Finally, the locks were all freed, and he struggled to push the doors open. He looked about as he did this, and all I could see were what seemed like large crates in the darkness inside. He pulled me into the building and then quickly closed the doors. I felt almost naked in the blackness and hoped I wasn't going to get conked on the head or something.

Suddenly a blaze of fluorescent lights shone overhead. I had to shield my eyes for a second. As I refocused my vision, what I saw astounded me. All along the central aisle of the building were hundreds and hundreds of cases of liquor piled high to the ceiling. As we walked down the aisle, I saw the names Johnnie Walker Black, Stolichnaya, Tanqueray, Canadian Club, and Wild Turkey.

We neared the middle of the building and turned left onto another long aisle where there were stacked cases of wine from Napa and Côtes du Rhône. Further along were crates of foodstuffs: jars of olives, dates, tomatoes, peaches, and pears. Next to these were cases of cigarettes and then a section of assorted groceries. The place was bigger than any supermarket I had ever seen.

CHAPTER 3

We turned again and, halfway down another aisle, we stopped. Mahommet opened the door to a refrigerated room and turned on a light that revealed cases of every beer brand in existence. *Heaven.*

"What brand would you like?" Mahommet asked impatiently.

"I guess…I guess maybe we'll try the Heineken?" With all the options, I had no idea what to ask for and was still in a daze.

"How many cases?"

I hesitated. "Well, I don't know how many I can carry back to—"

"I have a truck in back of the warehouse," he quickly interjected.

"Oh, er…well, how much will it cost to buy two cases?"

The five thousand piastres were, of course, highway robbery, but I didn't even flinch. We carted the beer to the truck and, ten minutes later, I was unloading them from the rowboat onto the stern of *Bravura*.

I entered the cabin with an air of casual triumph. Dick and Roger were both reading in low lamplight. They hardly looked up.

I hauled a case of the Heineken onto the table. "Here's your beer…There's another case out in the cockpit. And the diesel mechanic will be here sometime tomorrow." I turned and hauled myself into the compartment that Roger had showed me earlier.

Exhausted, I fell onto the bunk. What a first day on *Bravura!* I felt a bit relaxed after my coups of the evening and was glad that I would probably fall asleep quickly. But as I started to feel the waves of unconsciousness, I felt movement on my pillow. I switched on the cabin light and saw dozens of roaches crawling everywhere.

4

Day two on *Bravura* began uninspiringly. I had spent the night tossing and turning in my bunk because I thought the roaches, which I had had to get rid of by soaking my bunk with bug spray, would return. When I finally dozed off, I was awakened by loud exchanges between Dick and Roger. They had wasted no time digging into the hoard of beer I had bought and, by the middle of the night, they were pretty wasted. I wanted to hear what they were saying, but I was too tired.

In the early a.m., they were on deck doing repairs. I had finally gotten an hour of early morning sack time when the banging started. Awake and bleary-eyed, the first thing I did was check for more roaches. I didn't see any, so I hit the head and then went into the galley. I didn't understand why I was so hungry until I realized that, with all my nighttime wanderings, I hadn't had any supper. Roger came into the galley and without so much as a "good morning" or a "thank you" walked right by me and went into the head.

I felt squeamish about asking if there was any breakfast food because I had failed to fix the reefer. But after I thought about it for a few seconds, I decided that my late night achievements had more than made up for my mechanical ineptness. My annoyance at their ingratitude and Roger's brusque snub emboldened me. So, I went straight to the food cabinet, pulled out a box of crackers, and sat and ate some. I washed them down with some warm water from a half-empty glass and then went back into my cabin to get dressed.

"I'm not sure what time the diesel repair guy is going to arrive," I said, passing by Dick as I went up on deck. He stared back blankly and whispered something about "whenever he gets here." I noticed that he had parts of the reefer strewn about and was trying his hand at the repair.

"What should I get started on this morning?" I asked him.

Without looking up he said, "Guess you should ask Roger."

I walked around the wheel column and headed back into the cabin thinking that I'd better get used to the lack of friendly communication from these guys. On my way down, my gloom quickly returned as I envisioned weeks at sea with my two antisocial crewmates.

A few minutes later, I was moving boxes and stores from the forward cabin. When I asked Roger for a task, he said that the water pressure was really low and that maybe I could see if there was a leak in the pipe up forward. He never looked up from his work at the navigation table. As I moved the carload of heavy boxes, I wondered if, somehow,

CHAPTER 4

I was being written off by Dick and Roger as an unwanted commodity.

I heard some commotion on deck. Dick was talking to somebody with a thick Arabic accent. I hadn't heard anyone come aboard, so I dug myself out of the pile of stores and went up top to see what was happening.

The International Diesel repair service had arrived. My mood instantly brightened. Now we could get the hell out of this dreary anchorage and get the voyage going. Dick was jawing with the repair guy, and it wasn't going too well. He yelled forward. "Roger, can you talk to this guy? I can't understand what he's saying."

The guy seemed friendly enough. When I got up to the cockpit, he was looking around and smiling. He waved a greeting when he saw me, and I waved back. Roger had come close and was talking to him, but I couldn't hear the conversation. By the time I got closer, Roger was flailing his arms and shouting. "What do you mean you won't go down there?"

The guy said something back and instantly Roger lost it. "You goddamn people are impossible. This company's supposed to honor all requests for repairs on the warranty."

Now I was in the middle of the group. "No, no, no..." the guy replied, still smiling. "No warranties apply here. You must get new engine."

Roger was incredulous. "You mean you won't even go below to see what the problem is?" Now, he was really screaming.

Dick had walked away, so the guy turned to me instead, still smiling. "No, no," he said. "It is not possible. You need new engine." He put his hands out and continued. "Fifteen thousand dollars for new engine," he said, as if he was expecting me to give him the cash right then.

Roger had moved away but was still gesturing and cursing uncontrollably. The diesel representative was turning from him to me to Dick and back to me, looking for support. It was as if he was the injured party and we were bullying him.

I tried to calm things down and looked at him with my best rational face. "You mean to say that you came here all the way from Cairo, and you won't even go down and look at our engine?"

He smiled again as if I had given him support, but said, "Yes, yes, fifteen thousand for new engine."

After a few more of these ridiculous exchanges, I realized that I was in the middle of the old Middle East hustle once again. More screaming from Roger ensued with Dick tossing in his own to boot. "Get off this boat, you crooked son of a bitch" was the mildest of Roger's oaths.

As Roger and Dick moved toward the guy, he turned to me with a paper in his hand. "Please, please," he said. But this time he wasn't smiling. "I must get two thousand piastres for my consultation and cab fare." That was enough for me. It wasn't my engine or my boat, but I wanted to toss him overboard. The expression on my face must have gotten to him somehow because he flew down the transom and into his dinghy. He rowed rapidly toward shore but kept yelling out angrily. When he got to the shore, he stood up and shook his fist in our direction. He kept this up for at least five minutes. I couldn't understand his Arabic but was certain that he had convinced the other boaters and whoever was in earshot that we

CHAPTER 4

were gangster Americans and had completely victimized him.

"Well, what're we going to do about the engine?" I asked before returning to my work in the bow.

"We're just gonna have to wing it with the sails," said Dick. He seemed unfazed by what had happened.

Roger was looking at some papers. "The only other place where we can get the engine repaired is Malta. International is closing its operation there next month, but with any luck we should get there in plenty of time. But if we don't make it, we'll never get home."

As I made my way below, my gloom turned into real worry. The super sailors of *Bravura* might be used to this kind of stress, but this New Yorker is starting to sweat, I thought.

I went back into my hole and returned to the task of clearing the storage boxes. I kicked at the boxes wildly; I couldn't control my anger. And it was only the realization that I had reached the floorboards that calmed me down. I stood up and cleared a couple of half cases of rusted cans of soup away from the entryway. The bottom of the cardboard on the cases was wet and, as I pried open the hatch, I saw that the wood was heavily soaked.

I reached across the compartment for a flashlight and shone it below onto the freshwater pipe. I had a momentary catharsis. There, in the middle of the pipe, was a jagged hole with our supply of fresh water flowing into the bilge.

Well, the situation was not great, but at least I had uncovered the problem. I wanted to yell up to the guys that I had found the cause of the freshwater leak. Instead, I restrained myself. If they can be cool about the ups and downs of circumnavigating, I thought, then so can I.

I took a deep breath and shone my flashlight down to the hole in the pipe again. I was starting to wonder what had made the jagged edges in the hole when my heart skipped a beat. The biggest rat I had ever seen had crawled out of the aperture where I had been standing. I heard myself say "motherfucker!" or some equivalent expletive, and then I went into a homicidal rage admixed with bone-shaking fright. How I found a broom in the area I don't know, but I struck the creature as hard as I could. He was barely grazed, but my second blow got him on the head, and he squealed loudly.

I followed with rapid fire smashes in the throes of the only murderous spell I had ever felt in my life, cursing and screaming. I must have hit him several times after he was dead but couldn't stop myself.

The tension of the past days had caught up with me, and I had really lost it. My yelling had at last alerted the crew, and they came down to see what the commotion was all about. When they came up behind me, I turned and half pushed them away as I sat down. As I threw my broom across the settee, I saw my hands shaking. The evidence was there for all to see: the gnawed pipe, the water flowing, and the dead rat's brains all over the floor. There really was nothing to say.

The guys moved around a little while I kept my head down staring at the floor, trying to calm myself down. After a minute or two of watching me straightening the boxes and cleaning up the wet floor and the corpus delicti, Dick and Roger climbed the stairway, evidently realizing that I needed to be alone for a few minutes. As he passed me, Roger gave me a pat on the shoulder. He would never know how much that meant at that moment.

5

The next few days aboard *Bravura* were spent preparing for the next leg of her voyage around the world. As is always the case on long, blue water sails, there are always more tasks to perform than there is time to perform them.

I was particularly eager to get on with the sailing. I had had my fill of the Middle East and longed for the Mediterranean and the romance of Homer's "wine-dark sea." My latest gloom had come from the endless chanting of the daily call to prayer for Ramadan. Loudspeakers blared throughout the town and harbor of Port Suez, and the drone of the chanting penetrated through my skin to my bones. I didn't realize it at the time, but this would go on for weeks as we made our way up the Suez Canal and put in at small villages and ports for shelter and supplies. What I couldn't get over was the number of speakers. We must have heard thousands of them en route to the Mediterranean.

I tried everything to avoid the endless cacophony of the chanting. I played with every radio on the boat—VHF, UHF, satellite, AM, and FM—to get music from the outside world, but I got only static. I began thinking there was some kind of conspiracy. Thank goodness I had brought my tape recorder from home. But I had space for only a few tapes and wanted to save them for when we were at sea.

One of the most insidious problems aboard *Bravura* was the wind from the desert, which kept blowing sand onto the deck and into the cabin—even between the sheets. It wreaked havoc on the deck rigging and the gelcoat of the freeboard.

The day after the rat episode, I was in the dinghy alongside *Bravura* with scrub brushes, various soaps and cleaners, and a pail of water trying to clean the freeboard. I was struggling because the grime was thick. I distracted myself from the scrubbing from time to time by gazing out into the canal where a young kid was sailing his little dhow. He seemed to want to approach our formidable cutter, but we were flying the American flag, and he had fear in his eyes.

After about two hours of scrubbing, I took a break and popped open one of the few cans of Coke that we had left aboard. I stood up in the dinghy and raised the can to acknowledge him and called out for him to join me. He wanted to come closer but then thought better of it. He was curious but still apprehensive.

I went back to work in the sweltering heat. It was well over a hundred degrees Fahrenheit, and I continually doused myself with water to stay cool.

A few minutes later, I felt a pleasant breeze. What a relief, I thought. The breeze freshened, and soon I could feel the

CHAPTER 5

sweat on my back evaporating. It evolved quickly into a stiff wind. When I moved the dinghy around to the port side of *Bravura* where the wind was coming from, I saw that the sky had blackened. An empty paint can blew off the deck with a clang. By the time it hit the water, other flotsam was flying off in all directions. The wind started to howl as I climbed aboard *Bravura* and, as I whirled around, I saw the other boats in the basin heeling wildly toward us. Then a line snapped with a sound like a firecracker. What the hell was happening?

As Dick and Roger peered out from inside the cabin, I looked in their direction and threw my hands up in question. The anemometer on the wheelhouse read sixty knots—and the needle was moving upward steadily. *Holy shit!*

I crawled to the cabin entry, struggling all the way. As I turned aft, I saw two of the boats that had been tethered to the buoy with us flying past our stern out into the canal where a humongous oil tanker was passing through. The crews were desperately trying to steer their boats into a small embankment to avoid smashing into the tanker. I couldn't believe the scene in front of me. *Bravura* was now practically on her beam in a wild heel, with the anemometer now reading eighty knots. If our bowline severed, we would go flying out into the canal like those other poor bastards.

Then, with a suddenness that I simply couldn't comprehend, the howling died down and the beating wind ceased. I watched the anemometer needle reverse itself, as if someone was winding it down.

It couldn't have been more than forty-five seconds later when the sun broke through the blackness!

Instantly we were becalmed.

I stood up in a daze from my womblike crouch. "What the fuck was that?"

"Sirocco storm," said Dick with a matter-of-factness that pissed me off.

Big-time circumnavigator. He's seen it all and is playing it cool while I sit here scared shitless.

In a minute we were all up on deck in the hot sunshine surveying the scene. To starboard of us in the little basin, the two boats whose lines had severed had steered into the embankment and avoided hitting the tanker. That was the good news. The bad news was that they were wedged in the sand on their sides. One had its mast broken and the other's was bent in half. Even by my amateur estimate, it would cost a fortune to get them out of there, make repairs, and get them sailing. The rest of the basin was a total wreck with garbage everywhere, trees and plants uprooted, and an old car on the shore overturned.

And this had all happened in less than five minutes—from a titanic storm that didn't even bring a drop of rain.

Later on that afternoon, we all were busy trying to clean up *Bravura*'s decks when I remembered the Arab kid out in his little dhow. What had happened to him in the sirocco madness? I dropped my chores, went to the stern, and climbed out into the dinghy. Thank God I had tied the oars on, or they would have become flying missiles.

I rowed away from the flotilla of tethered boats and made my way toward the canal. I couldn't get too close to the shipping lane because a monster freighter or tanker might be right around the embankment. Although I wouldn't be directly in its path, the bow wave that these huge vessels churned up would easily be enough to overturn my

CHAPTER 5

dinghy. I kept close to the Egyptian shore that was a forest of swampy reeds. It was weird to look across the shipping lane that was no wider than Park Avenue back home. On the other side was the Sinai Desert where the Israelis had come across in the Yom Kippur War. I could actually see rusting cannons and a damaged tank opposite my dinghy on the other side. Once again, nobody had bothered to clean up the mess. It was just as littered as the desert stretch I had crossed when I'd come from Cairo to Port Suez.

I kept rowing along the Egyptian reed bank and spotted a tall stick a long way off. When I got to it, sure enough, I saw that it was the mast of the dhow. As I pushed the dinghy through the reeds, I had a moment of anxiety. Was the boy okay? But when I came up on the dhow, there he was in it, standing tall.

The only problem was that he instantly recognized me and was pointing a pistol at my head.

"Hey, hey," I said. "It's only me. I rowed out to find you to see if you were okay."

I quickly realized that he certainly couldn't understand English, so I put my hands up. I felt like an idiot, but what else could I do? I was thinking how embarrassed I'd be if anybody saw me surrendering to a little kid when he said, "I know you're the American in the big sailboat," in perfect English. He lowered the weapon but was still wary.

"Look," I said. "I'm not going to hurt you. If you'd like, I can help you get your boat from out of the reeds."

"I don't need your help." He was defiant.

"Okay, okay. I'll just row back to the basin." I lowered my hands, sat down in the dinghy, and rowed out of the reed bed, hoping he wasn't going to shoot me.

A NEW YORKER AT SEA

✻ ✻ ✻

Three days later, Roger came onto the boat in an animated state. He had been out since dawn but, in his usual incommunicative fashion, didn't tell anyone where he was going.

"I've finally got our clearance papers for the canal," he said as he climbed up the transom.

I couldn't understand why he was so wound up. After all, the boat had been in Port Suez for a couple of weeks, and I assumed such matters had been taken care of before I had come aboard. As it turned out, there had been an enormous amount of bureaucracy for *Bravura* and her crew during the voyage, and the problems in the Middle East were particularly vexing.

When I asked Roger what had happened, he alluded to the constant demand for *baksheesh*—or bribery—that he had encountered in dealing with the local officials. Of course, this didn't surprise me.

But that morning he had finally secured the last piece of the puzzle. In order to sail through the Suez Canal proper, a pleasure yacht needed to employ a licensed canal pilot. And he had finally secured one after a great deal of haggling.

"He'll come aboard at midnight tonight," said Roger, "and we can get moving again." Then he went below. I was as excited as I had been when I had first signed on for the voyage back in the United States.

The episode of the diesel mechanic hadn't really resolved itself. Roger and Dick had decided that we would just have to wing it to Malta. We would use the engine only when we had to and would have to rely on our sails if she cut out altogether. At best, Dick was going to have to empty out the oil pan very frequently, or the fuel injectors would get fouled.

Hopefully, when we got to Malta, which was over 1,500 miles away, we would get the professional help we needed at International Diesel.

This news had depressed me, but I hid it well. It was a practice I had begun during my fateful ride across the desert from Cairo. I had no choice but to continually bury bad news because, if I kept thinking about it, I would get into a terrible psychological state. Bad news had been the constant bill of fare since I had arrived aboard *Bravura*, so I had had a lot of practice. But in this case, practice certainly didn't make things perfect.

Yet, when Roger told us we were leaving that night, my whole body breathed a sigh of relief. The romantic notions I had carried during the years of my readings of great sailing returned so quickly, it was as if I had swallowed a magic pill.

The myriad chores that were left that day I tackled with an energy I didn't know I had. I scrubbed and swept and washed and straightened as I if had been three people, and even Dick blinked once when, in my cleaning frenzy, I almost knocked him down with a broom. He was also busy with his machine tools. He had figured out the problem with the reefer: it needed a new water-feed pipe. So, he was machining one. I was amazed at his great engineering skill.

Roger spent most of the day trying to balance the self-steering gear. Later, he asked me to sort out the charts that we would need as we moved north toward Port Said. I set the navigation charts out sequentially and pulled out the cruising guide. I circled the stops for food and supplies and noted the places the guide said we should avoid.

All during the day, as I had since I arrived, I watched the giant tankers, freighters, and container ships heading south in the Suez Canal passing within a couple of hundred yards of us. The rule was that ships could pass through the canal heading south during the day and north during the night. There was always a constant line of traversing ships.

The sight of these monsters, especially the oil tankers, turned my stomach. I couldn't shake the memory of the five hundred thousand barrels of oil spilled from the *Torrey Canyon* near the Scilly Isles. Fifteen thousand oil-slicked birds died in that disaster. Then there was the *Amoco Cadiz* that dumped over sixty-eight million gallons over two hundred miles off the Brittany coastline. Sixty-eight million gallons! My heart sank as I now watched the ominous tankers rolling through the Suez Canal, the odor of crude stinking up the air. The bastards.

As I sorted through the charts and maps, I re-studied the signal-sight systems that indicated the positions of these mammoth ships at night. They moved at high speeds, and there had been reports from yachties that they were ignoring radar flashers from pleasure boats and had actually collided with some sailboats. Money, and the tight schedules that made plenty of it for the oil companies, had become the new master of the sea; and the oil tankers were plowing through the oceans of the world, no longer caring about the small boats that sailed near them.

We were going to be near major shipping lanes when we struck out into the Mediterranean, and it was crucial to keep a careful eye on this large amount of commercial traffic.

CHAPTER 5

After my chores were finished, I dinghied over to two other sailboats that were tethered to the buoy. Even though I hadn't gotten chummy with the crews, I had acknowledged them several times and wanted to say good-bye. One of the vessels, *Gossamer*, was an aged ketch that was in bad shape. She was owned by an eccentric old Brit who I had privately christened "the ancient mariner." He certainly was as hoary and scary as Coleridge's hero and not at all sociable. He preferred sitting and drinking at dusk and shouting warnings to any of the local kids to stay away from his boat. I had called him "Captain" a couple of times and, when he answered me with "Matey," I figured that was as neighborly as he was going to get.

I rowed over to his stern and hailed him. He had told me his name was Mallachy—or Mallach. (He was hard to understand when he spoke.)

"Hi, Matey," he said, climbing out into his cockpit.

"I just wanted to say good-bye and wish you luck," I said.

"Where you headed?" he asked.

"We're going north out of the canal and then turning for Malta. I'm a little worried because our engine's not right." I didn't really want to tell him about it, but I guess I needed to get it off my chest.

"Want a tote a' rum?" He held out a bottle.

I certainly didn't, but he was being unusually cordial so I figured I'd humor him. When I stepped over the rail and into the cockpit, I was aghast. The interior of the boat was much dirtier than the outside. The cabin was a complete mess.

"Better check your weapons if you stop in Ismailia or those other coves near there," he warned as he offered me the bottle of rum.

"We don't have any guns aboard," I said. I put the bottle in my mouth and took a swig. It was the rawest alcohol I had ever tasted, but I didn't let on.

"Then you'd better not put in up there at all," he said. "Those Arab bandits always give yachties a rough time."

I thought about what he said for a second. "Well, hopefully we can win them over with a smile." He looked at me with a smirk. "And if that doesn't work," I said, "there's always baksheesh."

"Listen, Matey." He stood up ominously and pointed his finger at me. "There's only one way to deal with those bastards if they start up with ye. Ye've got to threaten them with any weapon ye got and tell 'em ye'll kill 'em." He roared the last words.

He was so intense that he started shaking. I didn't know what to say, so I took the bottle and downed another swig. I stood up. "I guess we can handle ourselves," I said with uncertainty and obvious fear in my voice. I climbed over the rail and back into the dinghy.

He grabbed my arm with his gnarled hand. "Just remember what ol' Mallachy told ye' about 'em." His eyes glittered, and his voice was portentous.

I shivered as I lowered myself into the dinghy. "Where are you headed?" I asked him, offering a smile and changing the subject. He looked out at the ships coming through the slot and then back down at me as I started rowing. He didn't answer but instead gave me a half salute and climbed back down into his cabin.

Back on *Bravura* Roger was attending the little charcoal burner on the stern rail and loading it with briquettes he had gotten from somewhere on his last scrounging trip. He

CHAPTER 5

had tried for fresh fruit, meat, and vegetables but had struck out completely. We'd have to stop somewhere up the canal for those items and for fresh water.

As he prepared to light the fire, I asked if I could do anything. "Yeah," he said. "You can scale those fish I picked up in town. We can celebrate our departure from this hellhole with the last of the beer you brought."

It was his first acknowledgment of my coup from that crazy night with Mahommet. I was glad that he seemed in a good mood. He was always so close to the chest with his comments that I was glad for a little insight into his feelings. Up to that point, I hadn't realized that he was unhappy with Port Suez, but I now felt a little better.

So, my captain hates this place as much as I do, I thought. I climbed down into the galley. But it sure made me feel a lot better about my depression. I got to work on the fish.

Later, I sat in the cockpit after having the best dinner since I had boarded *Bravura*. Roger had fried the fish with some flour he'd scrounged when they had first arrived in Port Suez. It was stale and tacky, but we weren't fussy. The fish was fresh, and we knew we were lucky to have it.

After dinner, the guys went below to get some sleep. Our pilot, whose name Roger said was Mustapha, was set to board at midnight, and we had planned to cast off as soon as he arrived. I returned to the cockpit after washing the dishes.

I was too excited to sleep. A three-quarter waxing moon was shining, and my mind contained exotic thoughts and adventurous anticipations. I looked out into the canal and watched a container ship pass through. Soon, I wouldn't have to stare at these big ships any longer.

53

I wanted to listen to some music on my tape recorder but resisted the temptation. We'd be at sea for a couple of weeks, at least, depending on the wind and weather; I decided to save my favorite sounds from home for the briny.

It wasn't until 1:15 a.m. that Mustapha finally showed. I had dozed off watching the stars and barely heard him climbing up the transom.

"Good evening. I am Mustapha, the official pilot for the Suez passage," he said ceremoniously. He was a swarthy, dark Arab with a barreled mustache that was carefully trimmed. His voice was deep, and he was smiling and in a cheerful mood. I welcomed him and offered to help him with any luggage, but he had only a small shoulder bag.

"Mustapha's come aboard!" I yelled out to Dick and Roger. It took them a couple of minutes to come out, which gave me a chance to size up our new pilot.

"You have a luxury yacht," he said. He sat back against the compass on the port bulkhead.

"Oh, watch the compass," I said.

"Oh yes, of course," he said awkwardly, feeling his way around the cockpit.

"Can I get you something to drink?" I asked.

"No, no, I am fine. Perhaps later." He took out a cigarette and lit it.

Dick and Roger came up and mumbled their usual perfunctory greetings to Mustapha. After a few tries, Dick started the engine, but I wasn't too happy with the sound of the ailing diesel. Roger went forward and released the line to the buoy, and we were free.

Dick was at the wheel, which made me a little anxious. The one thing I was confident about was my ability to

CHAPTER 5

steer a straight course at the helm, and I couldn't wait for my chance. In two minutes we were out in the canal and had turned hard to port. I looked aft and was surprised that there wasn't some monster ship coming up fast. But we were alone.

We were all standing in the cockpit looking back at the sorry yacht basin we had finally left. A slight breeze was up and we were motoring at about five knots. Roger and Dick were both focused on the oil pressure gauge. "Looks okay now," said Dick. "But whoever's at the helm has to check it constantly." Then he went below, leaving the wheel to Roger.

Roger looked at Mustapha. "Do you want to take the helm?" he asked.

"Oh no, no. You can steer the boat." Mustapha quickly sat down and spread his arms on the railing.

But I didn't miss my chance. "I'll take her, Roger, no problem," I said.

He hesitated. "Okay, she's yours. Just watch that oil pressure gauge, and keep her close to the green buoys."

I took the helm and feigned calmness. I tried to be casual and made sure that my hands were loose on the wheel as I adjusted the helm seat. My eyes darted from side to side, and I made sure I was on the starboard side of the passageway.

I was offended by Roger's comment about the "green buoys"; it was a bit terse and condescending. Any amateur would know to keep his course there, but I guessed that he was showing me that he still didn't have much confidence in my seamanship. I didn't have that much confidence either, but I sure as hell could steer a straight course.

Then Roger went below, leaving me and Mustapha in charge.

I liked having my charts right next to me when I was at the helm, and I passed the time away by checking them and looking for the next course marker. The canal channel was easy, of course, but I knew there were marker buoys every kilometer; I immediately started looking for the first one.

After about ten minutes of silence, I tried small talk. "Have you been a pilot long?"

Mustapha didn't answer. He was smoking and staring ahead. I repeated my question much louder. He couldn't ignore it this time. He flicked his cigarette butt into the water. "I have done this for two years. I also do other things." He still avoided looking at me and seemed irritated at my question.

I checked the charts and watched the buoys. There was sufficient light in the cockpit from the compass nightlight and the instrument dials. I also had a small pencil flashlight that I had brought from home. As long as the generator worked, we would have power for all our electric appliances—reefer, lights, instruments, and radios. But, of course, it all depended on our crippled engine.

It was going to be another twenty miles before we got to Shandur. After that, the canal area would widen out into Little Bitter Lake and then Great Bitter Lake, and maybe then we could raise the mainsail and shut off the engine.

I was continually apprehensive about the damaged diesel. I imagined the worst. What if the engine quit suddenly and a big ass oil tanker was right behind me? I would have to turn hard to port, head for whatever land mass lay ahead, alert the crew, and then slow down the boat before it hit the beach or dock or whatever I was headed for by tossing

CHAPTER 5

out the small stern anchor. I rehearsed all of this a couple of times.

After about two hours running, my stress abated. The diesel seemed to be okay as I checked the oil pressure gauge for the hundredth time, and the boat was moving steadily at four and a half knots.

I had desperately needed to hit the head an hour before but had held off. Maybe now I could risk a quick trip into the cabin. "Mustapha, I need you to take the wheel for a moment."

He turned to me quickly. "I am a canal pilot. I do not steer the boat."

"Mustapha, I need to go below for just a minute. Please take the wheel. I'll be right back." I moved away from the helm letting go of the wheel with one hand. He couldn't refuse this minor request. I saw his fists clench as he fidgeted nervously as I went below.

I felt the boat turning back and forth unnaturally as I stood in the head peeing as quickly as I could. *What the hell is he doing up there?*

I stopped prematurely and raced back up to the cockpit. Mustapha resembled a person trying to steer a bicycle for the first time and, seeing me, left the helm before I had a chance to grab the wheel.

I took control and was relieved that I didn't have to jerk the wheel back on course and wake up the crew. I wanted them to sleep peacefully and not have to worry because the amateur from New York was steering the boat.

When everything returned to normal, I thought about Mustapha. Canal pilot? If this miserable son of a bitch was a canal pilot, then I was Christopher Columbus. Even a first-time passenger on my sailboat back in the Hamptons could steer better. Who the hell was he? Should I call Roger and Dick to tell them that our canal pilot was a phony? I got angrier and antsier as I reflected on yet another instance of local skulduggery.

Eventually, I calmed down in the blackness. The canal was getting wider as we got closer to Shandur. Someone was stirring below. Roger came up out of the cabin disoriented. "Where are we?" he asked.

"We're two miles from Shandur." It was a deliberate response with planned precision. I pointed ahead. "You can see the channel widening out up there to starboard."

"Need a break?"

"Sure." I checked my watch. I had been at the wheel for four hours. "I'll try to get a few winks. Call me if you need anything." I went below feeling pretty proud of my first watch.

I decided not to tell him about Mustapha. I didn't want to be the one always crying "Mommy." I wanted to be just as blasé as my crewmates. I wanted to appear as a hardened a seaman such as they were. When Roger found out about Mustapha, as he was bound to, I wanted to be the one who, upon hearing the bad news, shrugged his shoulders with the tacit reaction of an old salt who'd seen it all.

6

I actually slept for quite awhile and awoke only when I heard arguing above. I'd been dreaming about someone shooting at me and woke in a sweat. When I looked around, my quiet cabin yawned back at me, and I realized things were in order.

I went to the head and then climbed the steps to the cockpit. "I'm not giving you any more money," Roger was yelling. His neck veins were bulging red.

We were docked on an old quay, and the sun blinded me as I looked up at Mustapha. He was standing on the quay pointing an accusatory finger at Roger. "I will report you to the harbor police. I am official canal pilot, and you cannot treat me this way…"

I wondered what Roger had done. While Mustapha kept up his babble, Roger was tying up some figure eights on a winch and had turned his back on Mustapha. I could see from the look on his face that the discussion was over.

Mustapha kept provoking him for another minute but then calmly picked up his shoulder bag, walked purposefully onto the beach, and left.

"Where's he going?" Dick asked coming into the cockpit, scratching his head and pulling up his shorts.

Roger didn't look up. "He's leaving. He claims that his jurisdiction ends here."

"What are we supposed to do for a pilot the rest of the way to Port Said?" I blurted. The shrillness in my voice gave me away. Once again, I sounded more like a panicked landlubber than an old salt.

"The bastard claims that his brother will replace him tonight and accompany us the rest of the way. But I don't believe him," said Roger, who was oiling a winch.

The sun was really blazing now, and the heat was bearing down. Roger looked over at me. "Maybe you can take a walk and scrounge around up over there," he said, pointing to a high plateau where we saw some shacks. "I'm getting concerned about the water supply, but we also need food."

I hated the idea. "Sure!" I said, and quickly went down to get my topsiders and some piastres.

I climbed onto the scorched earth and began to trudge. The sun was relentless. I had walked about a half mile in the blistering heat and had seen no one. The cruising guide had had no information on Shandur, so I wasn't surprised. I turned up what looked like an old path and came up on a rise from which I was able to see some shacks. I walked down to them quickly. I could see that there had been a town there once, but it had been bombed out like the areas in Port Suez.

CHAPTER 6

I saw some movement and a few people wandering but had to keep shading my eyes from the burning sun. I walked through some old streets and turned up one, which was more of an alley. Here the shacks were close together. I was hoping one of them might be some sort of store.

I had to clear away some rotted fence posts and other garbage as I poked my way along, feeling depressed.

Then I saw a woman running toward me with wild eyes and fear on her face. Behind her were two guys with clubs swinging wildly and shouting. One swing had struck the woman on her shoulder. She screamed and, as she ran past me, I tackled the two guys without hesitation, yelling at them to stop. Their faces showed their surprise. At one point I picked up a garbage can cover and flailed it at them. They fell back, but they were still cursing me as I tried to shield the woman.

I was livid. What the hell could a defenseless woman have done to these guys to warrant them trying to club her to death? I took another run at them with my stupid garbage can cover and, finally, they stopped cursing and pulled back. All the yelling had drawn a crowd—from where I didn't know. The people started milling about and, although I couldn't understand what they were saying, it seemed that they were taking sides.

Half were with me and the rest were against me. I started to move back; I wanted to get out of there because no good was going to come of this for me. The woman seemed to be okay now that the neighborhood had gotten involved.

As I turned back toward the water, a battered jeep pulled up and a guy that looked like a cop got out. He started jabbering with the crowd and then turned to me and said something I couldn't understand. *Here we go. Now I'm in trouble.*

I squared myself up and walked closer to him, looking at him straight in the eye.

"I'm an American," I said. "I come from a boat on the canal. I was looking for a store to buy water when this woman ran by me with these men chasing her."

He put his hand up. "Be quiet," he said in clear English. He turned and started talking to the crowd. The two club carriers pushed their way through and vigorously started talking to the cop. They were gesturing wildly toward me.

Finally, the cop turned to me and asked for my papers. I took out my passport and opened it. He took it from me and leafed through it. Then he talked some more to the crowd. He turned back to me, flustered. "You have interfered in a family problem," he said. "The men want me to arrest you. They are the husband and the son of the woman."

I couldn't believe it. I wanted to say, "How the hell was I supposed to know that these guys were her family?" But I didn't. I took the cop by the arm and walked away a few paces. I told him I was on an official boat that was doing important work for Egypt. I said I didn't want any trouble and was going to return to my vessel. I would not tell any of the officials I saw what had happened.

The cop immediately backed off. He gave me back my passport and turned to the crowd, motioning for them to break up. They didn't waste time.

He softened his demeanor toward me. "My friend, you must not interfere with the family rules of our people."

I interrupted him and told him I respected the practices of the people and wouldn't dream of interfering. *Blah, blah,*

CHAPTER 6

blah. At this point, I didn't care about anything but getting out of there.

I finished up with him by saying that all I was doing was trying to buy some water.

He looked around and then surreptitiously took my arm and led me to the jeep. He opened the back door and pointed inside. "I can sell you some water. Four hundred piastres for each bottle. How many do you want?"

I just shook my head and took out the money. "I'll take the whole case," I said. There were six pint-sized bottles. Not hiding my disgust, I tossed the money at him, picked up the case, and trudged back to the boat.

I finally got back into *Bravura*'s cockpit and sat down feeling beaten. "What took you so long?" Dick was sorting out sail grommets. I looked at him hard and then went down into the cabin. To hell with it, I thought. I'm not going to tell them a thing.

Roger twisted the knife in my back when he yelled from the cockpit. "Is this the only water you could find?"

✵ ✵ ✵

It was just after midnight when Mustapha's brother Ahmad appeared from nowhere. He announced his identity and asked if we had any Hershey bars. Dick and Roger wouldn't give him the proverbial time of day, so I extended greetings to the newest member of the Suez Canal Pilot's Association (a.k.a. Mustapha and Ahmad's family).

Unlike his brother, Ahmad was talkative and jovial. However, when I offered him the helm shortly after we motored out of Shandur, he politely declined and moved away from the steering column with the swiftness of a Nile asp.

I took the first watch as my crewmates slept. Initially, I was grateful for Ahmad's garrulousness but, as he began to turn an account of his life into a plea for soap, cigarettes, or anything else I might possess, I got crazy. I told him that his family had already swindled us by breaking the agreement we had had with Mustapha, who was to guide us the entire length of the canal. He countered by smiling politely and telling me that we had misunderstood the terms of the agreement. I knew I couldn't win with him, so I told him that I had to be quiet while I consulted my charts.

I was jolted out of my socks when a large horn sounded and, in the same instant, a beam of light shone onto our stern. At first, I thought it was a big ship, but the vessel quickly pulled abeam of us; it turned out to be a police boat. The crew was shining flashlights up and down *Bravura* and was draped in automatic weapons. Now what? I didn't know whether to cut my engine or what. Roger and Dick had torn out of the cabin and were shielding their faces from the flashlight beams. Any decision I was about to make was cut short by a cop with a bullhorn. "Good evening, my friends," he said. "Welcome." He was smiling, and his voice sounded sincere.

We quickly waved back expressing friendship, more or less. I made sure I had the biggest smile I could muster. Dick and Roger could have done much better, I thought, as I waved and smiled enthusiastically.

"Do you have any biscuits or sweet candy for us?" he asked. The bullhorn echoed across the water.

CHAPTER 6

Roger had by now grabbed our bullhorn from the cabin door shelf. "We have nothing here. We've given our last baksheesh to the pilot thieves," he said.

I was pissed. This was not the way to respond to a gunboat with machine guns aimed at us in the middle of the night, in the middle of nowhere.

The cop withdrew his bullhorn and barked something to his crew in the wheelhouse. The flashlights were aimed at us as the boat moved closer. For a second I thought they were going to ram us but, as they got within ten yards, they went in the opposite direction, accelerating rapidly. The huge wake they made caused *Bravura* to tip way over on her beam. As I struggled to right her, the gunboat roared off into the darkness. They had evidently decided we weren't worth any hassle.

Roger went below mumbling obscenities, with Dick trailing behind him. In two minutes the water was quiet again, and it almost seemed as if the whole incident hadn't happened.

Okay, so we couldn't escape this plethora of stressful happenings. But, I thought, as I tightened my hands on the wheel, soon we'd be out of this goddamn canal and away from this madness.

Even before this latest intrusion, I had planned our next stop on the east side of the waterway—in Israeli-occupied Sinai. I thought we could get some food and water over there without any hassle. At the end of Great Bitter Lake, which we were now moving through, there was a marker on the map for a water tower and a small settlement.

All along the canal, we had seen the vestiges of the Yom Kippur War of 1973. In October of that fateful year, the

Egyptians had launched a surprise attack on Israel crossing the Suez Canal with one hundred thousand troops, armor carriers, tanks, missile launchers, and heavy artillery. Initial success in the Sinai was theirs, but after about four days of heavy fighting, the Israelis had hurled them back across the canal and had themselves taken up positions on Egyptian soil. That had been enough for Anwar Sadat and, very quickly, a negotiated peace prevented further hostility.

As we made our way northward up the canal, we spotted the rotting weaponry of the conflict. The iron and rubber pontoons that both armies had used to cross and re-cross were still on the banks of the canal. Scattered about were the remains of tanks and armored cars. Occasionally, we saw unexploded shells and abandoned missiles in the sand.

As I steered *Bravura* through the war-torn area, I imagined what it had been like during that hellish time with dismembered bodies flying through the air, the whizzing of missiles above, and the explosion of artillery shells. The Middle East was so filled with such intense hostility that war could break out once again in a flash. Not a pleasant thought as I motored through the night.

Another train of thought entered my head. The reason so many of these people despised Americans was that we had failed miserably in convincing anyone that we were for a fair peace. We had entered into secret agreements with wealthy Arab oil sheiks, yet continually supported the Israelis while turning our backs on Palestinians and other desert peoples. The result was that, in the '80s when I had traveled with my students to the Mediterranean, terrorism increased—and so had anti-Americanism.

CHAPTER 6

I looked up at the American flag on our transom pole, swelling and fluttering in the sea breeze. Then, I looked over at Ahmad and wondered what he thought of us Americans sailing in our expensive pleasure boat through his homeland, while many of his countrymen were impoverished.

All of this contemplation of the world situation might provide fodder for a healthy discussion in my classroom back home, but it did little to boost my morale sailing through this ravage and ruin.

My reverie was interrupted by Ahmad, who decided to renew his campaign for more baksheesh. Once again, he appealed to my sense of pity by describing the woeful poverty he was undergoing. After a few minutes of listening, I told him to be quiet because I thought I heard the sound of a boat. I was mistaken, but some peace had returned to my steering pedestal.

A fog had settled on Great Bitter Lake. It wasn't rolling in like the soup over the Atlantic back home, but it was beginning to affect my long-range vision. I slowed the engine down a knot and looked at the oil pressure gauge, which was reading normal. I couldn't understand it because the engine had been running for three hours. Maybe the gauge was malfunctioning. Maybe Dick's diagnosis of the injector problem was inaccurate. Maybe we were going to be okay. Or, maybe the engine was going to die, leaving us helpless in the path of an oncoming oil tanker. My mind churned.

This was all typical in long passage making. There were always uncertainties. There were always contingencies to consider. There was always something to stress you out.

I kept straining my eyes in the fog, watching for any sign of the water tower area on the Sinai bank. I kept close to the green buoys on my starboard as always. I kept checking my charts and recalculating the theoretical distance to the water tower. It was supposed to be one hundred feet tall, so I should have been able to see it from a distance.

I watched the time carefully and kept the wheel dead on course. I had heard stirring in the cabin and, shortly after, Roger came up into the cockpit. He looked around at the foggy lake. "I'll take it for awhile," he said. Normally, I would have been grateful for a blow, but I resented this abrupt takeover. I had worked hard to get us to our destination, and now my efforts were being usurped.

"Sure." I grabbed my flashlight and gear and stomped my way down into the cabin. I wanted to show Roger that I was pissed, but then the thought occurred to me that, from his perspective, there was no reason for me to be annoyed. Why would anyone be angry upon being relieved after a tedious watch? Perhaps my behavior was getting erratic. Was I starting to lose it? Was the strain of one misfortune after another finally getting to me? Was I totally unfit to withstand the rigors of such a voyage?

I got into my bunk and tried to relax. Then I turned on my nightlight to read. Since we had the engine running, cranking the generator, it was alright to use electricity. But my mind wandered as I tried to read; I couldn't stop reflecting on my mental state. Finally, I turned off the light, closed my eyes, and tried counting long, deep breaths.

I had gotten to eight when I heard Roger above. "On deck! On deck!" he yelled. It was the emergency call for assistance. I jumped into my shorts and shoes and was up there in a flash. I was glad to see that Dick was still lagging below.

CHAPTER 6

"I thought I saw the tower a few seconds ago," he said. "I can't see it now, but I also heard what sounded like horses running. And the water depth is decreasing pretty quickly."

"How far back was the last marker buoy?" I asked.

"I haven't seen one since I relieved you."

I grabbed the night glasses that were on the steering pedestal and pointed them toward the Sinai shore. I blinked and doubted what I saw, so I put them to my eyes again to be sure.

"Yeah, yeah, the tower's right over there." I pointed on a forty-five-degree angle. "Cut the engine or we'll pass it." I felt triumphant that Roger had to obey my direction.

We slowed down and turned to starboard, leaving the channel. Ahmad had been nervously squirming around the cockpit. "I am afraid of going there," he said. "Please do not take me there." He sounded pathetic.

By now Dick was on the port beam with a powerful spotlight that he had hooked up. "I think there's a small dock over there," he said. "Somebody get a line..."

I pulled some dock line out of the starboard locker and ran up to the bow along the starboard railing. I coiled up the line so I could lasso it to whatever protuberance I could find. I stood up, waiting to spot the dock in the fog.

I heard what sounded like snorting but still saw nothing.

Dick was moving the searchlight beam back and forth along the waterline. Except for the sound of the diesel, all was tranquil as we slowly approached our fogged-in target.

Suddenly, a wall of men on horseback appeared directly in front of us. They lined up near a tiny pier that jutted out a few feet from the embankment. Roger had seen the embankment and instantly put the engine into neutral.

Idling now, we saw a dismounted horseman on the pier just ten yards from the boat. The breathing and snorting of the horses was the only sound. The riders were shabbily dressed but they wore bullets crisscrossed over their chests and rumpled cowboy hats atop their heads.

If I hadn't known where I was, I would have sworn I was in the presence of Pancho Villa and a bunch of Mexican bandits. I wanted to swallow, but my throat was parched.

The "bandito" on the dock took off his hat and smiled. He extended his arm and said, "Let me help you with your boat." He spoke in an accent I recognized. I had heard it for weeks on the Egyptian side of the canal.

There I was standing on the bow with the line in my hand, and he was now within a few feet of me. I looked at the group of gunmen on the horses in the blackness and knew we were in serious trouble. There was no one else around, and we were completely defenseless.

I don't recall what was going on in my mind. But suddenly, I looked at him squarely. "If you even touch this dock line, I will kill you where you stand." I used my loudest, most threatening voice and wound the line around in the air in as menacing a manner as possible.

He actually took a couple of steps backward. I seized the opportunity. "If you don't get out of our way, we will destroy you here in the MIDDLE OF THE NIGHT!"

My body was shaking violently, but I kept spinning the dock line wildly in the air.

He bolted. He jumped on his horse and he and the entire mob retreated, turned their horses around, and rode off into the night.

CHAPTER 6

But I stood there spinning the line around in the air and screaming into empty space. Dick finally came over to me, put his arm around my shoulder, and brought me back to reality. As we walked back to the cockpit, I remember Roger spinning the wheel rapidly as the engine roared in reverse. By the time Dick helped me down the steps to the cabin, we were chugging full speed back into the center of the waterway.

I lay in shock on my bunk. My body wouldn't stop shaking. I kept thinking about what Mallachy had told me about how to treat the unscrupulous brigands of the canal. I thanked him repeatedly, as if he were sitting next to me. After awhile, I must have fallen asleep.

7

When I awoke, I felt the boat moving but didn't hear the sound of the diesel. I moved around on the bunk for a minute or so and then slipped on my shorts. I climbed the steps and saw Dick at the helm. I looked toward the bow and, for the first time, saw *Bravura*'s mainsail and genoa unfurled.

"What's happening?" I asked Dick.

"Had to shut down the engine. She was burning oil," he said. "We're trying to sail a bit through the rest of the lake until we get to Ismailia. We need a lot of motor oil, not to mention water and food." He looked more alert and uneasy than I had ever seen him.

"Where's Ahmad?" I asked.

"He jumped off as soon as we got to the Egyptian side last night, after you scared away those guys on the horses. You sure saved our asses."

He was dead serious. I didn't say anything but realized that it was the first time anyone had acknowledged that I had done something important on the voyage.

Later, when Roger had come into the cockpit and we were all munching on the last of the stale hardtack, Dick said, "Well, I sure didn't think there were outlaws on the Israeli side of the canal."

Roger furrowed his brow. "It doesn't make any difference which side we go to. There's gonna be somebody wanting to grab this boat and get rid of us. Thank God Joe freaked out last night and scared off those guys or else we might be lookin' at Davy Jones right now."

I felt a surge of pride at what Roger had said, but it was fleeting. I realized the implications of what had occurred. The truth was, no matter what side of the canal we were on, no matter what religion or belief dominated the people, this was the desert and there were cutthroats and pirates everywhere, ready to pillage. They would try to scam us, humiliate us, threaten us, and maybe even kill us. The important thing was to get the hell out of there as fast as we could.

Unfortunately, our situation looked bleaker than ever. We were headed for Ismailia, which the cruising guide had warned to avoid at all costs.

Yachties had reported that thievery, violence, and the worst of the zone's corrupt officials were in this town. But we had no choice. Our engine was down and, without it, we couldn't get to Port Said. As it was, we were contravening the rules, which prohibited raising any sails in the canal waterway. At any moment, a patrol boat could shoot out from a mooring and haul us in. Our pilot had jumped ship,

CHAPTER 7

but no one would believe or care that we had actually hired two who had both scammed us.

We could do nothing but make for the town, which was actually marked with a skull and crossbones in the cruising guide. Somebody had had a macabre sense of humor.

We busied ourselves by cleaning and tending to our usual myriad chores. Roger was at the helm, and twice we had to tack out of the way of ships coming at us from the north. We were not even supposed to be heading north in the daytime, much less sailing.

As we approached the town of Ismailia, we hauled down the sails at the closest distance we dared, and then motored on in. It was my first chance at hauling down the main, and I was surprised. The sail weighed a ton, and it was no easy task for two men—Dick and myself—to fasten it properly around the boom with bungee cords. As we worked to get it down, I imagined how difficult it would be to do this in heavy weather.

Luckily, we accomplished our task without being detected by the police. Roger had started the engine, the oil pressure was holding for the moment, and we motored on in to the little harbor. We looked around for yachties, but there weren't any. They had all given the place a wide berth following the dictate of the cruising guides. We slowly motored around looking for a place to tie up and finally found a spot next to an old tugboat.

We tied on lines fore and aft and were attaching a spring line from the port side when we saw a brigade of uniformed men marching toward us. "Now we're in for it," said Roger.

They came to a halt right in front of the tugboat. The leader had plenty of ribbons on his uniform blouse, so it was apparent that these were military men rather than local gendarmes. Looking down at *Bravura*, he put his hands behind his back and paced back and forth. I caught his eye and smiled, but he didn't return it.

"You have documentation for this vessel?" He was talking to me in clear English.

I pointed to Roger and said, "That's the captain." Roger kept the boat's papers handy in the cabin door shelf. He reached down and then handed them up to the officer. I had a bad feeling about this, but I noticed that my mood wasn't as black as I imagined it would be. We had been through so many struggles in the past weeks. Was I getting used to these crises?

The officer was speaking in Arabic on a portable radio that was pressed to his ear. He had his back to us but, even if we could see his face, we couldn't understand what he was saying. He was taking a long time, and we could do nothing but stand around. I was thinking of offering the soldiers some cigarettes from the packs that we had left in our baksheesh stores. There was always a catch when you thought about doing this. You might be reprimanded for trying to bribe an official or maybe even be arrested. Or, upon seeing your stash of baksheesh, the officials might board your vessel and clean you out.

We waited and waited. The wind picked up as the skies darkened, and I thought we might be in for another sirocco storm. But it quickly died down, and the sun once again flashed its hot rays from behind the clouds.

After long minutes had passed, the officer turned to us as he pushed down the antenna on his portable radio. He bent down and handed the boat's papers to Roger. Then he

CHAPTER 7

stood erect as he looked at the boat and then at us. And then, he turned and walked away with the soldiers in lockstep behind him.

Holy Toledo! We looked at each other in disbelief. I was so ecstatic that I couldn't hold back this time. "Wahoo!"

Roger and Dick shook their heads and sat down.

Without thinking, I climbed onto the dock and ran after the soldiers.

I ran past the column of soldiers and caught up with the officer. "Please, excuse me, sir," I said, trying to keep up with him. He stopped and I continued: "Officer, we are in an emergency situation with our boat. We desperately need motor oil for our engine—and water and food. Can you *please* help us?"

He looked at me but said nothing. Then, he turned to the soldiers and yelled something. A soldier fell out from the rear, ran up to him, and saluted. The officer took him aside a few steps and mumbled a few sentences. Then, he turned and barked orders to the column and they marched away, leaving the one soldier.

The soldier turned to me. "I am Muhammad," he said. "What is it that you need?" His accent was thick, but I smiled at him not hiding my excitement.

"Muhammad." I shook his hand vigorously. "I am Joe. I need supplies for my boat. Where can we buy motor oil and water?"

At first he didn't understand, and then he put his hand up and said, "You come." I nodded and we started walking. I stopped abruptly realizing that I didn't have any money.

"Wait, Muhammad. Come back to the boat with me." I hooked my arm through his, and we turned back to *Bravura*.

I locked my arm in his as we walked. I wasn't going to let this guy get away.

By the time we had returned from *Bravura* and were walking toward wherever Muhammad was taking me for help, I had gained what I thought was a measure of amiability with him.

With a combination of sign language, broken English, and halting Arabic and body language, we were communicating pretty successfully. He understood that my first priority was motor oil but that we also needed water and food. When I had rushed back to *Bravura* for money and quickly rejoined Muhammad, the crew had called after me. "Try to get some beer!"

Those ungrateful bastards, I thought, as we walked toward what I now perceived was a fairly large town. If it weren't for my hustling we would be high and dry without anything. But now that I've connected, instead of thanking me, all they can think of is their precious beer.

After a twenty-minute walk in unbearable heat, Muhammad brought me to a garage where motorcycle tires and car parts littered the landscape. He spoke to a scrawny guy with a cigarette dangling from his mouth. He looked like the head grease monkey, and Muhammad appeared to be making fast headway with him. The grease monkey was nodding and bowing agreeably, and I began to think that I had struck gold with Muhammad.

They both walked back to me, and the proprietor took me by the hand into a supply room. There stacked against a wall were dozens of cases of Castrol motor oil.

My mind raced. How could I get back to the boat with a bunch of cases of this stuff?

CHAPTER 7

I asked them right away how much it would cost. They spoke and, after a little haggling with the guy, Muhammad had obviously triumphed. He turned to me and quoted a price that was so low I couldn't believe it. I tried to hide my wild excitement and then asked if ten cases could be delivered to the boat. Muhammad didn't have to negotiate this but simply said, "Yes, yes."

I turned away and started counting out piastres. Emboldened, I motioned to the proprietor to load the oil onto his truck. By now I had established enough authority so that I didn't need Muhammad to translate. The guy bowed to me and carried the cases to his truck.

My mind was now in overdrive. Smiling, I told Muhammad that we needed to stop for water and food, and could we please use the proprietor's truck to stop at a store on the way to the boat?

Muhammad understood all of this quickly, and I was amazed that he didn't balk at all at my impudent hustling.

An hour and a half later, Muhammad, the proprietor, and I were back at *Bravura* with a truck so loaded with supplies that it took Roger and Dick a half hour to load it onto the boat. I had gotten five cases of canned food, fifteen-gallon jugs of water, ten packages of bread, some dried meat and fish, dozens of candy bars, three jars of peanut butter, and five cases of beer—in addition to the motor oil.

Even Roger and Dick were impressed with this mother lode that I had scrounged, even though they didn't drown me with praise.

The most incredible feat of all was that I had paid retail! While my crewmates carried the supplies, I brought Muhammad and the proprietor down into the cockpit, sat them down, and offered them every item I could think of for refreshment.

They gingerly accepted some soda and cigarettes but, as I flooded the cockpit with items, the proprietor kept pleading with Muhammad that he couldn't eat or drink because of Ramadan. Evidently, Muhammad didn't have quite the same spirituality because he partook more freely.

As dusk settled, my guests indicated that they had to depart, so I walked back to the truck with them, thanking the proprietor repeatedly in every language I could conjure for his immense hospitality and graciousness—words that I hadn't thought of in a long time.

I took Muhammad aside while the proprietor said goodbye to Roger and Dick. I put a very large wad of piastres in his hand. I got teary-eyed as I thanked him.

He smiled and hugged me in friendship. Then, he said, "Joe, my friend, I cannot accept this money. Please understand." He must have felt badly at seeing my wide-eyed disbelief.

"Muhammad," I pleaded. "Please, please accept this gift of thanks. My God, you saved our lives by what you did this afternoon."

He gently pushed away my hand that held the money. "I cannot," he said. He hugged me once more before he climbed into the truck. "Have a good voyage."

As the truck moved away, I ran to the passenger window. "Muhammad, I will never forget you." He smiled and waved as the truck sped off.

I stood in the roadway and found that I could not fight back my tears.

8

That evening, even the normally pokerfaced Dick and his equally dispassionate cohort Roger could not restrain themselves. They jauntily prepared a meal of hamburgers, potatoes, and canned peas. I got into a festive mood myself, set the table in the cockpit with extra care, and poured their beer just before the meal was ready.

I poured myself a Coke. It was the first I'd tasted since Cairo, and I really savored it. I raised my glass. "Well, here's to our luck changing for once." The guys joined in—albeit with less enthusiasm than the occasion warranted.

I persuaded them to talk a little about the first parts of *Bravura*'s voyage. They had had two other companions aboard and had great success photographing reefs and World War II wrecks for a magazine. The boat had performed excellently, and their voyage had been undisturbed. "It's only since we got into this goddamned Middle East that we've been snake bitten," said Roger.

"Yeah. You brought the evil eye with you, Joe," added Dick.

I looked over expecting a jocular expression, but he was dead serious.

"Ah, well," I said sarcastically. "At least the age-old superstition of sailors at sea hasn't invaded *Bravura*." I resented their accusations. The two-against-one atmosphere was still present.

"I wonder what evil eye was responsible for the supplies I got back in Suez or the windfall I snared today," I continued. They were silent as they gulped down their beer.

I cleared away the dishes after dinner and brought them down into the galley. We had fallen into the routine of me washing dishes while Roger did most of the cooking. Dick occasionally dried them but, otherwise, disappeared into his cabin in the bow.

As I washed the dishes, I heard the conversation in the cockpit become slurred as the boys chugged down their beer. Afterward, I went into my cabin and spent some time straightening up and getting my dirty clothes into a pile. Then the voices up top changed. I stopped straightening to listen.

"I just want you to know, Roger, that I hate your guts," Dick was saying. He sounded pretty drunk. I wished I could see his face. Roger didn't respond right away, but I heard bottles being knocked over, and then, "I wish I could throw you overboard, you jerk."

To say the least, it was disturbing to hear my crewmates showing such contempt for each other, even if they were drunk.

CHAPTER 8

The unspoken but strictly adhered-to rule was absolutely no drinking at sea. But in port, Roger and Dick had hit the sauce like two alcoholics. They had never displayed any real animosity toward each other, but the drunken exchanges on this night were strange.

My guess was that the long stretches they had spent together at sea had produced some negativity. I reflected back on stories I had read about sailors behaving weirdly and eccentrically after prolonged voyages, about how violence had broken out due to the strain and constant tension.

Roger and Dick were certainly not the most sociable companions, but it never occurred to me that they might become violent. I sure hope I don't have to referee a wrestling match out at sea, I thought, as I prepared myself for bed. I cursed the fact that the only nice day I had had aboard this vessel was ending on a note of unpleasantness.

We decided to finish our Suez Canal run without hiring another pilot. After the fiascos of Mustapha and Ahmad, Roger felt it would be a case of throwing good money after bad, and I couldn't really disagree. We would, of course, take the risk of being stopped and fined—or who knew what else—but the risk was worth it. Besides, we were just about out of piastres.

It was a straight canal run from Ismailia to Port Said. The plan was to head out of the harbor at Ismailia and idle for awhile just before our sharp turn to the north. We'd use our binoculars to look south and wait for a long stretch between ships. Then, we would go. We were taking a chance that the engine might start acting up, but Dick had topped her off with fresh oil. We now had spare cases if the oil problem got worse. We wouldn't be able to run the engine when we got out into the Mediterranean, but we were, after all, a superb sailing craft and would be able to handle just about anything in open water. We'd have to be careful with our satnav and any electrical appliances, but we'd manage.

After getting about three hours of sack time, we arose at 2:00 a.m. and eased out of our slip. I hadn't slept well. I was eager to get going and finally be part of the open water experience of circumnavigating. I had read a little but had to turn off my nightlight so as not to waste the battery. I lay in the darkness, forced to listen to the sacred wailing from the loudspeakers of Ramadan. It was so unnerving that I had begun stuffing toilet paper in my ears. Well, this would be the last time I would have to hear it.

We motored as quietly out to the channel as we could. Dick was at the helm and Roger on the bow. As soon as he was able to see the slot to the south, he put his binoculars on and focused in. Almost immediately, he turned to Dick and me in the cockpit and gave us the prearranged signal to turn hard to port and rev up the engine to cruising speed.

He crawled back to the stern along the foredeck. "There's a ship about a mile back. We should be okay if we can keep our speed up." He put the binoculars on the steering pedestal, but I removed them quickly and focused them northward. I couldn't discern any ship lights in front of us whatsoever, and I said so. If all went according to plan, we would pass the center of Port Said at about 9:00 a.m.

With all of us in the cockpit, we motored on. No one was interested in sleeping during this hoped-for final leg of the miserable Middle East. The night desert air was cold, as

CHAPTER 8

always, so after an hour of motoring, I volunteered to make some hot coffee. I actually got a "thank you" from the crew.

Unfortunately, although this might have been an ideal opportunity for some pleasant pass-the-time conversation, my cohorts were in their usual state of glum silence. I tried some provocative commentary on the politics of terrorism and the terrible stalemate of the Middle East power struggle, but it didn't stimulate any talk from the taciturn duo.

As I sipped my coffee, I turned around to look at the ship on our stern. "Uh oh," I said. I pointed aft and the guys turned around. "The lights are much nearer than before," I said. All eyes were on the speedometer, and it was dead on five knots per hour.

"That's supposed to be the speed limit in the canal," said Roger.

"Well, that baby's going a lot faster than that," I said, nodding toward the monster gaining on us.

Roger throttled up the engine to six knots. We chugged along as the waterway widened just a bit and continued to see the scattered weapon remnants of the Yom Kippur War. The outskirts of Port Said began to appear as "rosy-fingered dawn" and lit the shoreline.

I looked back and, sure enough, the ship's lights in our rear were getting brighter. "Goddamn it," said Roger. "That bastard must be doing seven or eight knots. Why doesn't the shore patrol give *him* a summons?"

In the terse conversation that followed, Dick and I agreed that the big ships pretty much had their way in the Suez Canal and also in most of the oceans and major waterways of the planet. The ancient tradition of the sea, where small sailboats were given the right of way, was rapidly disappearing. In addition, oil tankers disregarded antipollution efforts everywhere. I told the guys that I had taken pictures of a tanker emptying its bilge with oil and debris in the middle of Long Island Sound a few summers back when I was ferrying a small sailboat from New York to East Hampton.

The bitching and moaning about the monster commercial ships taking over the world continued. But I realized that this conversation was detracting us from a more pressing problem: the monster to our rear was about to overtake us. "Hey, guys. I don't want anyone to panic, but that tanker is moving up on us pretty fast. What're we gonna do?"

Roger turned around again, cursing. He moved the throttle up a knot.

"Can't rev up any more," said Dick. He had gone down to the cabin to check the engine. "I'm smelling oil like crazy down here, and the engine is getting hotter."

"The oil pressure gauge is reading pretty normal up here," I shouted down to Dick.

"I don't give a crap what the gauge is readin'," he yelled back. "The engine is overheating." Dick had climbed halfway up the cabin to make sure we understood the urgency of this situation.

"Well, it's going to be a race to the mouth of the Med," said Roger. "We're going as fast as we can. He'll have to run us down right in front of the population of Port Said if he wants to pass us."

I agreed with Roger's assessment but, as I turned around and stared at the Leviathan getting ever closer, I feared for the worst. I thought about one of the most sinister sea stories I had ever read, *The Ship Killer* by Justin Scott. It was

CHAPTER 8

about a giant freighter that runs down a sailboat and kills the owner's wife.

We were now even with the center of Port Said and it seemed strange, after snaking our way through tiny towns and villages, to be near a large city. It would have been natural to motor over to dockside, tie up, and walk to the nearest coffee shop and have breakfast. But here we were without an official canal pilot, so we didn't dare for fear of having our boat impounded or being arrested.

I looked to our rear for the hundredth time and gasped. It would be a close call. Roger was steady keeping the boat close to the green channel buoys on the starboard side of the passageway. He didn't seem nervous and didn't turn around to see how close our pursuer was.

Bravura started to hobbyhorse a little as we entered the end of the canal waterway, where the small chop of the Mediterranean current met up with us. Every few seconds the vista on our bow widened as we came up to the end of the African continent and headed north to European waters.

The deafening sound of the loudest horn I had ever heard reached our ears. *My God. He's right on our ass*. But, as I wheeled around, I saw that he wasn't really. My estimate was that a quarter mile still separated us. But that didn't matter to the monster ship. It was well known that if these commercial ships slowed down even a bit, their profit margins would slip and all hell would break loose in the company's executive dining room.

No, it didn't matter to the monster that we were going to be well out of his way so that he didn't have to slow down. Even the slightest possibility that he might have to slow down for a crippled sailboat was enough to make him sound his horn at us.

The sound was so deafening that I noticed people on the shore stop and look out into the canal, even though they had probably heard horns like this all the time; they lived adjacent to the busiest artificial waterway in the world.

Amazingly, we were now out of the channel and into the Mediterranean. And now the oil pressure gauge was definitely in the red zone. "Let's raise the main in a hurry," said Roger, looking straight out to sea and disregarding the ship.

Dick and I moved like scared rabbits, undid the bungee cords, and started to haul on the halyard. Halfway up, the already-grinding task of pulling got worse; a stiff breeze from the west had come up quickly after we had moved out of the canal.

We had practically hauled both of our bodies up the mast trying to force the heavy mainsail to the top but were only three-quarters there. "Turn the goddamned wheel into the wind or we'll never get this sail up," Dick said to Roger. He had a look on his face that I had not seen before.

"Can't do it," said Roger. His tone was calmer than the situation warranted. "I can already feel this bastard's bow wave coming toward us. Pull that halyard for all your worth."

Dick and I couldn't see how close the ship was because we were facing the bow and pulling with all of our might to hoist the sail. Inch by inch we battled and, finally, looked up to the top of the mast and she was up. We flew to the cleat and figure-eighted the halyard. We collapsed at the base of the mast, catching our breath, when we saw the tanker suddenly on our port. She sped by us; her bow wave was flying toward us and appeared ten feet high.

CHAPTER 8

"Oh boy. We're in for it," said Dick.

But *Bravura* didn't heel that badly as the wave struck our beam. The guy at the wheelhouse was high up the wall of the ship, and the son of a bitch didn't even look down at us to see what was happening as he roared by and headed out to sea.

"The *Harry S. Truman*," I said, reading the name of the monster on her stern. How ironic. One of our more appealing presidents. I wonder what he would think if he saw a ship that was so ruthless named after him.

In a flash, we had averted an accident, furled our mainsail, and were leaving the dreaded Middle East. I leaned on the mast for awhile and watched Port Said fade on our stern. Dick had quickly hauled up the jib from the cabin as soon as the tanker had passed us. We were now heading west-northwest with a steady twelve-knot wind at our port beam. *Bravura* was liking the set of her sails and gliding nicely through the water.

For a moment, I felt exhilarated. I was on a terrific cutter sloop that had sailed halfway around the world, and we were entering the waterway where Odysseus had sailed ages ago. We had beaten back the scammers, thieves, and outlaws of a very unfriendly part of the world. We were finally free from fear. And, at last, I didn't have to listen to those miserable loudspeakers wailing out the call to prayer.

✧ ✧ ✧

After a few hours we began to settle in. Unlike our haphazard custom in the canal, we would now be taking regular watches. I would be at the helm from 6:00 to 10:00, both a.m. and p.m. In between I would have some chores but also a generous amount of free time. I had carefully planned how I would spend this time.

In addition to some select reading, I wanted to hone my navigational skills. I had had a little instruction in using a sextant and working out the tables to plot our course using the popular noon shot of the sun. The more difficult moon shots and use of the fifty-seven navigational stars would require lots more practice. To complement this, I had extracted a promise from Dick that he would help me learn the sat-nav procedures. I had always been a curmudgeon with new technology and very impatient with instruction manuals. I also resented the dictates of the capitalists who were constantly hurling new gadgets at me and, when I steadfastly resisted, was told that I was "falling behind."

In addition to these tasks, I would review the light signal systems to track commercial ships because we were right in the middle of some of the busiest shipping lanes in the world.

After downing a peanut butter and jelly sandwich, I retired to my bunk and relaxed after our harrowing hours passing through Port Said. Dick was on watch, and I had a couple of hours before my evening shift at 6:00 p.m.

I had gathered some new navigational charts in my cabin and had started to trace our course from the mouth of the Suez Canal to Malta—a distance of about eleven hundred miles on the rhumb line or straightest course. Of course we would have to tack occasionally, depending on wind direction. We would pass Alexandria and then the Libyan coast on our port and sail under the southern coast of Crete on

CHAPTER 8

our starboard. As I viewed these locations on the chart, I recalled the names of some ancient sites in this part of the Mediterranean: Knossos, Mycenae, and Carthage. Significant historical and mythological tales had evolved from these places and great literature written to commemorate them.

And then, *BANG!*

I heard what sounded like an explosion on deck. I arose quickly and started shaking. What had happened now? I struggled with my shorts, hit my head hard on the bulkhead, and raced to the cabin steps. I had climbed two of them and could see the sky from where I stood. But it wasn't the sky I saw; it was the black freeboard of another ship.

At the top of the stairs I saw Dick calmly standing at the wheel with the ship passing off our stern.

"Sorry," he said. But he certainly didn't look contrite. "Uncontrolled jibe. I didn't see that ship because I was blocked by the mainsail. The jibe sheared the track block, but we're okay now."

I had experienced a couple of uncontrolled jibes—a sudden swing of the mast boom from one side of the boat to the other—on my boat *Typee*. The biggest danger occurs if people are standing up in the path of the boom. On a small boat, they can get a rude conk on the head. On a large boat, they can easily get knocked out and tossed into the water. It's caused by a sudden swing of the wheel or turn of the tiller, often to avoid a collision.

That is exactly what happened to Dick. He was sailing along with the mainsail blocking his vision of what might be coming toward him on the port side. In that situation, one has to constantly move by ducking underneath the sail or by taking some steps forward to get a quick peek of whatever might be coming from behind the sail. Dick had failed to do that.

He only saw the ship when it was too close and had to change his course, instantly causing the jibe. But unlike a small boat boom, *Bravura*'s boom was so large and heavy that the instant swing sheared the track block, a solid piece of steel hardware the size of a brick.

I looked at the sheared block and couldn't believe the force that the swinging boom had exerted. The boom was high enough so that it swung over Dick's head. If it had struck him, he might have been decapitated. It reminded me of the difference in forces between a small boat and a fifty-two-footer like *Bravura*. When a line or a sheet slips on a small boat, one can usually grab onto it and prevent it running free. But when such a line slips on a boat like *Bravura*, one has to let it go or find oneself suddenly in the ocean.

I had read about all of these pitfalls in various sailing stories through the years, but when they actually happen, the stress can be so severe that I have to wonder what good it did reading about the experience.

The cumulative effect that these misfortunes had on me was very negative. Because I had to maintain a degree of alertness that was highly intense and because my nerves were worn out from the memory of so many incidents, my state of mind was dominated by constant worry.

As days at sea wore on, I found it more and more difficult to enjoy the romance of the sail because the image of a disaster waiting to happen was always lurking in my consciousness.

I tried hard to push the bad memories away and focus on the good things that were happening. The more snafus

CHAPTER 8

and breakdowns that occurred, even the minor ones, the more difficult the battle. When the stress became too great, often a feeling of hopelessness would come over me and depression would set in. I questioned why I was even on such a voyage and wondered if I had lost a measure of my sanity.

The countless tasks that had to be undertaken aboard the boat were, ironically, a psychological boon because they forced me to take my mind off this inner struggle.

✫ ✫ ✫

When the time came for my first official watch in the open sea, I tried to be as prepared as possible. I had brought my own harness with me from home and, after relieving Dick, lashed it to the railing. As I did this, I remembered the stories I had read of helmsmen swept overboard because they weren't wearing their harness, or they had momentarily unhitched it because they wanted to move forward atop the cabin to adjust a line or untangle a snarl.

I had brought the navigation charts, the light signal system manual, some foul weather gear, and my tape recorder with selected tapes. I looked about with the binoculars and saw a ship far off behind me. I squinted at the setting sun in the west, which was our course. I donned sunglasses and, after a few minutes, sat down on the steering pedestal seat. *Bravura* had self-steering control, so I didn't have my hands at the wheel. We had decided to employ the self-steering, which consumed a small amount of electricity, as long as we would not drain the battery.

The southwest wind, which had carried us out of Africa, was still blowing steadily at about ten knots so that I could keep *Bravura* directly on the rhumb line course of 280 degrees. I was very glad of that because, if the wind held up, I had a chance of beating Dick's watch distance of sixteen miles.

Despite the anxiety, stress, and worry that I had had, I still retained a strong competitive instinct that I had developed through the years of my urban existence. I was grateful for it because it gave me a measure of confidence. This confidence was of course continually being challenged by adversity and the various calamities. It was also challenged by my ineptitude and any remarks of my performance by my crewmates. So, I was glad for my competitiveness and, as I urged on the boat to keep up speed, made a playful toast to Poseidon and took a slug of water from my bottle.

As darkness set in, I became aware that this evening's 6:00 to 10:00 watch came with a bonus. Roger and Dick were fixing up dinner, and I didn't have to get involved because of my helm duties. A dinner plate and glass of soda were passed up to me, and I felt like royalty even though the dried potatoes and canned meat were tasteless. I could see the guys eating but couldn't hear their conversation.

As I ate, I stared at the sunset and a rush of emotion entered into me. The wide expanse of sea and the sun against the backdrop of stratus clouds was spectacular. Just then a flock of birds flew overhead, moving north toward Europe. They added a wonderful, aesthetic touch to the scene, but I couldn't identify their species and became frustrated.

CHAPTER 8

I tried to settle back and enjoy the ride. This was what I had journeyed so far to experience, what had lured Moitessier and Slocum and other modern circumnavigators out to sea.

It was particularly amazing to witness sunsets at sea because of the endless horizon and serenity that that brought. As I gazed outward, I thought of the great sea writers—Melville, Conrad, Homer, and Masefield—and reminded myself how successful they had been in transforming their experiences for readers.

The next indulgence I had planned was music. I connected my earplugs to the tape recorder and heard the pulsing piano of Oscar Peterson. In addition to the indescribable rhythmic and melodic infusion that I experienced listening to great jazz, there was always the acceleration of idea association and transformation. I thought of home, naturally, and all the exciting happenings that were occurring in the concert halls, nightclubs, restaurants, museums, and galleries of New York. I thought of all the wonderful artists and performers.

I listened to the tapes for over an hour and, during that time, had escaped into the world of romance and fantasy. Not once during the hour did my anxiety or stress enter my consciousness. When I unplugged my headset, I smiled gratefully and thanked the inventors of the technology.

Just before I had turned off the music, I had noticed the jib luffing a bit. After putting away the recorder, I grabbed the winch and took in a couple of turns on the jib sheet. The luffing ceased, but I suspected the wind direction might be changing and checked the wind speed indicator. The steady southwest breeze was waning fast and backing around.

This activity was, of course, a predictable part of any cruise, but it annoyed me. I wished that I could hold my course on the rhumb line for another twenty-five minutes until my evening watch ended. I didn't want to start maneuvering the boat around on a new course, and I didn't want to call on my crewmates for assistance. I wanted my watch to be seamless. I looked at the tachometer and realized that I had just a half mile to go to beat Dick's distance; so, I hunkered down determined to do just that.

A few minutes later, I looked at the indicator and saw that the boat had slowed down by almost two knots. In addition to shifting to the south-southeast, the wind was indeed dying down. Even if I adjusted sails, it would do little to change matters. The wind was everything, and when it died there was nothing one could do, except start the engine and do some motor sailing if a rendezvous had to be met. Naturally, this wasn't an option for me.

In the next instant, I felt a gust of wind against my right ear. It had come from the east and was followed by a few more small gusts. Quickly, it freshened and started to blow steadily from the southeast. I had a moment of anxiety but soon realized that things would be fine if I just jibed the boat. Easier said than done! I wasn't sure if I could keep the boom from moving too far. I inserted the winch handle in the socket and kept turning slowly. Then I disengaged the self-steering control and grabbed the wheel. I changed course ever so slowly and stretched to keep the winch handle turning.

Just before the jibe, I let go of the winch handle because I was stretched too far from the steering wheel. As a result, the jibe was more violent than I wanted.

CHAPTER 8

By the time the jibe ended, the wind had picked up ten knots, and the main was sheeted too close. I uncleated the sheet rapidly—too rapidly. Instantly, the wind had blown the sail, and the sheet was flying off. I went to grab it but hesitated for a second, remembering that the force might send me flying.

Although matters were rapidly getting out of control, I made a decision to try and grab the sheet rather than call for assistance from below.

I clutched on desperately with both hands and felt them burn as the sheet tore through my hands. But in a few seconds, I had it tight and lunged to get it to the winch. Finally, I got two turns around the winch and was able to figure-eight it to the cleat.

I looked around wildly and grabbed the wheel just before the boat turned errantly. I straightened her out and got back on course. By the time I had done this, I realized that I was shaking again.

I took a few deep breaths and assessed the situation. I had successfully executed the course change and reset the mainsail, but I had failed in asking for help. If I had lost the sheet in the wind, then we would have been in a real pickle.

As it was, we were sailing along faster than before, and I saw that I had beaten Dick's distance. The wind had intensified to seventeen knots when a light flashed below and Roger was climbing up to relieve me.

"How we doing?" he asked in his usual impassive way. He looked around and saw that we were on a new tack.

"No problems," I said casually. "Wind has shifted and come up a bit," I added unnecessarily.

He looked at the twenty-knot distance I had on my watch. "Hmmm," he said. "Nice run."

That dumb little compliment was enough for me. I put my head down, gathered my gear, and kept silent. I wouldn't utter a word about the madness that I had undergone a few minutes before. I wouldn't whine about the fright and desperation I had endured. I wouldn't reveal the rawness in my hands from the sheet burns. No, I would keep all this to myself.

Instead, as I descended the stairs, I saw Roger struggle with the wheel as the wind intensified and the seas deepened. "You okay?" I asked. I was so glad to be out of this lousy new weather. I was hoping that he would ask me for some help. "Yup," he answered, staring out at the blackness.

I reflected on my actions as I huddled in my bunk trying to get warm. I had unknowingly gotten pretty soaked from the chop during my jibe episode. I was thinking about my ridiculous need to hide my fear, not talk about my hairbreadth activity, and not risk a critical comment about my stupid decision to go it alone up there. Why would I get so crazy if, once in awhile, there might be a chance that I could be perceived as inept or afraid?

9

I turned my psychological restlessness over and over in my mind and decided that some of it was pretty irrational. And if rationality was so important to me, why was I unable to resist wallowing in some of my emotional quagmires?

Thankfully, I soon fell asleep from the exhaustion of my watch and stopped my internal wrestling.

I slept for five hours even though in whatever dreams I had had, I could feel the boat fighting some pretty rough seas. After grabbing some orange juice and leftover coffee, I went up on deck to discover Dick at the helm, annoyed.

"How's it going?" I asked, sipping my coffee.

"Wind swung around to the west on Roger's watch, and he had to tack thirty degrees off the rhumb. That's where I am now," he said without emotion.

"Can I get you anything?"

"Nope."

I sat down and looked at the seas, which were a bouncy six to ten feet coming in on the port bow. Beating to windward was not a fun ride for me, and I began wishing that it would veer by the time I came on my next watch.

I sat for a few more minutes thinking that Dick would appreciate my company, but he said nothing. I would have been grateful for some conversation in the middle of the night, but Dick seemed almost put out at my presence.

I went below, grabbed a couple of butter cookies, and went back to my bunk. I thought about our tack way off the rhumb line and got a little fidgety. Unless the wind cooperated, our comfortable window of time to arrive in Malta would shrink. On the other hand, we still had a fairly nice ten-day cushion, and the odds were still definitely with us.

I wanted to play my tape recorder but decided to save it for my watch. I tossed and turned for an hour but couldn't sleep, so I took out my copy of Ian Fleming's latest, *You Only Live Twice*, and escaped from the voyage, the wind, the wrong compass course, and my antisocial sailing mates.

About an hour before my morning watch, I put my novel down and began playing with my sextant. The sky had brightened, so I thought that we might have a sunny day. Perhaps I could shoot the sun at noon and figure out our course and speed the way the ancients had for centuries.

I prepared my foul weather gear and got out a fresh pair of socks from by duffel bag. I made my bunk and straightened out the cabin. According to my watch, I still had a half hour to go before I relieved Dick. I was antsy. It wasn't that I wanted to be on the dewy deck and get salt water splashes from the windward course. What was it then?

CHAPTER 9

It quickly dawned on me that what I wanted was something basic, like picking up the telephone to call a friend. I chuckled. Of course I had known that I couldn't do this for quite some time now. Why, then, did the urge strike me at that particular moment?

At five minutes to six o' clock, I gathered my gear and trudged up to the cockpit. Dick was still on a starboard tack from the rhumb line but, when I looked at the compass, it had moved from thirty down to twenty-five degrees away. The sky was fairly clear, and the stars were still visible. I found myself wishing I had real sextant skill because there were a couple of good navigational stars waiting to be shot.

I dropped my gear and sat down, waiting for Dick to hand over the helm. I suddenly remembered that I had forgotten to say "good morning" when I had come up but awkwardly felt that, now, it was too late.

Dick picked up his gear box. "Wind's been holdin' for the last half hour." Then he let go the wheel and left the cockpit.

I reached for the helm; I didn't have to make an abrupt correction as he had expertly oversteered before he took his hands away. I was a bit jealous of his gesture but quickly committed it to memory so that I could perform this cool maneuver when I left the helm.

I checked all of the instruments while I settled myself into the pedestal seat. I felt the sun's warmth on the left side of my face and looked about for boats. There were three ships far off my port heading away and what initially appeared as another sailboat way off to starboard. I anxiously kept my eye on the spot while I looked at the compass heading and checked the self-steering control. After awhile, I recognized that the sailboat was just at the angle of the sun hitting the waves.

The water was sporadically splashing over the port railing, so I shifted my body to starboard. I started to reason that maybe the wind had crept up to the north a little and, if I adjusted the self-steering, I could get the boat closer to the rhumb without touching the sails. With small effort, I achieved my goal and got the compass over to just ten degrees off the rhumb line.

I was quite proud of my feat when I saw that the cutter sail was luffing a bit. I had hated this sail from the outset and could never understand why the boat needed it. Two or three times I had checked the speed indicator when it had been raised in the lee of the jib and, each time, the indicator remained steady. No increase in speed, and we had had to break our chops raising her.

I wanted to let the damned cutter keep luffing, but the flapping would drive me nuts. And if one of the guys saw it like that, I would get the evil eye. I had to unhook my harness but, because the boat was steady, I walked over to the sheets and took another turn around the winch. The cutter wasn't super tight, but if I wanted to keep my new course this would have to do.

As I turned aft to return to my seat, I saw a marvelous sight. There, just twenty yards from my transom, was a school of dolphins arch-diving and chasing the boat. They were a smallish gray species and were sporting the wonderful grins on their snouts that I had seen in countless films. I sat and stared.

The creatures were having a ball, or at least that's what it had always seemed like in the movies. I looked around and

CHAPTER 9

wondered how big the school was and what schools of fish they might be chasing.

The school was swimming symmetrically in a path about two hundred yards wide and stretched as far back as I could see. I tried to follow the movement of one in particular but, after a few tries, couldn't be sure if I had. My mood instantly lightened; I was so thrilled with these wonderful companions of the sea. Plato had once written about their wondrous activity, and many writers had described the awe they inspired. I must have stared aft at them for twenty minutes before I turned around to check our course, instruments, and steering control. My thoughtlessness brought on a moment of panic but, thankfully, everything was okay.

When I turned back to gaze at the school, their symmetry was starting to disappear. I sensed that they might veer off and leave me for some lousy baitfish. I wanted to chase after them but I couldn't.

I had another idea. I could try to feed them...

I ransacked the cabin for anything appetizing to throw into the water. I grabbed a box of cookies and then spotted the garbage bags that had been festering. I ran back out and flung the garbage aft as far in the air as I could.

Nothing.

They were really heading off to port now, so I broke off pieces of butter cookies as fast as I could; I tossed the crumbs at the straggling dolphins. Once again, my food was ignored.

By now they were a long way off and, as I strained to see the last of them, I was exasperated by my return of melancholy.

As they disappeared, I thanked Poseidon for the boon and realized that I had killed an hour of alone time. I hadn't had to turn on my tape recorder or bury myself in the navigation charts and maps to kill time.

I looked at the northwest sky ahead and spotted some wispy cirrus clouds that had formed during my game of tag with the dolphins. As I gazed at them and traced their pattern, I smelled something. It wasn't an artificial odor like cooking or my old friend, the rat. I couldn't figure it out and thought I was imagining it when I felt a shiver and realized that it had suddenly gotten colder. I stood up to zip up my foul weather gear and espied something a long way off the bow. In seconds I was in a panic.

Coming toward me all across the horizon were churning whitecaps. Fierce weather was headed my way. What should I do?

The sails had to be quickly slackened but, this time, I wasn't about to handle the situation myself. For a couple of seconds I rehearsed my call for assistance.

"Some bad weather headed this way, gentlemen," I shouted into the cabin. "Better get up here!" I cursed Poseidon. This damned Mediterranean! The weather could sure be temperamental here.

The wind hit us like a wall of concrete, and the self-steering control noisily disengaged. I ran for the wheel and tried to get my bearings. I could do nothing about the flapping sails and wanted to yell out "Get the hell up here!" to my mates. I didn't care that I would destroy the aura of veteran seamanship that I had worked so hard to cultivate.

Waves of green water came over the bow. I think I was about to cry "Mommy" for the crew when they scampered up from the cabin. Once they saw me fighting the wheel to keep the boat from broaching, they grabbed the sheets and started hauling like mad to take down the sail.

After taking the main down halfway, they expertly reefed her to the boom. I was so impressed with their reefing that I calmed myself and focused on the jib. They uncleated it while fighting the wind that nearly tore the sheet out of their hands. I knew that I had to steer more into the wind so that they could roll in the furling halyard. I struggled to do this as the waves wanted to push me sideways, but I slowly got her into the wind.

I was about to claim victory when Roger and Dick both flashed me a stern glare. I had made the right move, but I hadn't done it fast enough was the unspoken but unmistakable message on their faces.

I strained at the wheel and got the boat into the wind a few seconds later. But it wasn't going to stay there unless I oversteered back and forth. The instant I got her straight and the jib began luffing, the guys pulled on the roller halyard and, inch by inch, took in the jib. All the time, I was fighting the wheel and the waves.

They had taken in the jib so that only a handkerchief section was still sailing and rapidly cleated the sheet and halyard. At once, the boat responded, and I was able to steer much easier.

We now had a shrunken sail area, and the boat was taking on the boiling sea with authority. But Dick and Roger sprang out of the cockpit after cleating the jib, unlatched their harnesses, which shocked me, and crawled up the port side to the cutter sail halyard. They uncleated and hauled in the sail so quickly that I had to correct my steering. Now the boat was slicing through the water like a knife through butter.

The guys gathered up the cutter sail, which was flying all over the bow, opened the forward hatch, and stuffed the sail into the bow. Quickly closing the hatch, they crawled back to the cockpit, looked around at the huge swells, and climbed back down into the cabin without so much as a nod to me.

The whole maneuver had taken them less than ten minutes, and they had accomplished their task without breaking a sweat. For them it had been just another storm on their voyage around the world. I had to admire them.

All through the commotion, I had not paid attention to the wind speed indicator which, as I now peered over, was reading forty knots and gusting up to forty-eight. I was dumbfounded.

The boat was conquering a force eight gale in high seas with aplomb. *Bravura* actually seemed to like the conditions now that she had had her sails trimmed by her crew. Feeling the hull slide through the waves, I had a new respect for sturdy boat construction. *Bravura* had been built in Taiwan and had received plaudits for her construction from sail magazines. Now I knew why.

The hatch board sprang loose and Roger hopped up into the cockpit and grabbed the wheel. "Go get some dry clothes on," he said. I obeyed the order and went below.

I got out of my foul weather gear and found that I was soaked to the skin. How in hell did Roger know that?

I had bought a new outfit in New York before I left. I chose the Rolls-Royce brand of gear because it had long since received legendary homages from all the magazines. Well,

CHAPTER 9

so much for the hype from the advertisements and sales personnel. Not only had the water forced its way through the slits and seams, but it had also pierced its way through the fasteners. I cursed the manufacturers.

I changed my clothes, re-donned the foul weather gear, grabbed some butter cookies, and rushed back out into the storm. I waited for Roger to turn the wheel back over to me. "I can't reconnect the self-steering control," he said. "You'll have to keep the wheel. Make sure you stay on this course."

I actually said, "Aye, aye, Captain," and slid into the pedestal seat.

After Roger went below, I looked at my watch. I had less than an hour left on my watch. For an instant I was disenchanted. I was eager to experience the storm again because I felt safe with the new sail configuration and the stability of the boat. I wanted to get used to this foul weather so that when another storm sprang up, I could behave as fearlessly as Roger and Dick.

I noticed that the swells had lessened. I looked at the wind indicator and, sure enough, the wind was registering twenty-eight and dropping.

What? I kicked at the bulkhead and cried out to the wind something like, "Keep blowing you son of a bitch!" As I steered, I thought about what I had shouted. What the hell was wrong with me? Was I actually hoping that the storm would continue?

I laughed. I had a flash of the mad Captain Ahab and his insane desires. For just a moment, I had entered into his consciousness. "Oh, brother," I said. (I had found that I was given to talking to myself quite a lot while on watch.)

By the time Roger had come up to relieve me, the wind had died dramatically. He grabbed the roller furling halyard and unfurled the jib to its full breadth with only one hand. I was actually able to let go the wheel and help him unstrap the mainsail from the reef points. He went up to the bow, opened the hatch, and pulled out the cutter sail. He hanked it on the stay and hauled it up by himself.

I got my wet gear together and then looked at the distance traveled. I froze. After all that exertion, I had made only eight knots on the rhumb line.

Because of the storm, we tacked way off course, but I hadn't realized how much. *All that hassle, and for what?* I went below feeling thoroughly defeated.

Although I was pretty fatigued, I fought to read my spy novel. There was plenty of light in the cabin, so I wouldn't have to turn on my nightlight. After less than an hour, I dozed off but woke up suddenly from a dream. I had been scuffling at the wheel, and my harness came loose. A sudden wave had cast me overboard...

In a grumpy mood, I picked up the sat-nav manual and went through the instructions. I had read through the first five steps and had to re-read it because the instructions were so confusing. According to the manual there were six satellites and, if the unit was set up properly, an operator could get a navigational fix every forty-five minutes or so when one flew overhead. I decided to stop at step five and consult with Dick.

I went up to his forward stateroom and listened at the door. He was moving about, so I knocked.

"What is it?"

CHAPTER 9

I opened the door. Dick's cabin was a pigsty. Books and magazines were strewn everywhere on the bunk and floor. Among them were dirty clothes piled everywhere and bits of food caking up on the dresser.

"Hi. I was going through the sat-nav manual. I wondered if I could turn on the unit and play with it for awhile?"

"Sure." His eyes didn't leave the dime novel he had been reading. "But don't leave it on for more than a few minutes. It eats up the battery."

He turned on his side away from me, a clear signal that he wanted to end the conversation. I uttered a weak "thanks" and closed the door.

"A few minutes," I said to myself. "What good is that? How do I know when the satellite is going to be close overhead?"

I went over to the nav station and spent ten minutes straightening up the mess that Dick had left. I re-cataloged the charts, folded the maps and stored them in the correct sequence, and cleared away food scraps. I wiped down the surface with a kitchen cloth and then fetched the manual. I put it on the table, switched on the nav light, and re-read the manual again before I turned on the unit.

When I pressed the power button, nothing happened. No lights. No sounds. I checked the manual, looking at the diagram of the unit. I had followed the damned instructions to the letter. I checked the power cord. I repeated the procedures five times and still nothing.

I cursed the world of technology. Every fucking time that I had opened a box with a new radio, phone, toaster, or other appliance, I got the same results. There was always some confusing information to derail me. My patience had never been great, but I was particularly crazy around instruction manuals.

After taking deep breaths and trying another half dozen times, I quit. I was frustrated because I really couldn't bother Dick again, who was now getting ready to go on watch. I decided to ask him later on when I relieved him for my evening watch.

I passed the rest of the time restlessly reading and snacking on those damned cookies. I felt trapped by my inability to be productive with the sat-nav, by my failure to get any distance on my last watch, and by a creepy feeling of loneliness.

To hell with it. I grabbed some more cookies, took out my novel, and went up on deck. Too bad if Roger didn't want company. I was going topside.

The sea was unbelievably calm. The sky was hazy, so I couldn't make out the horizon. The sails were flapping even though Roger had everything set up properly. I went up amidships to the mast and stood there looking ahead as far as I could. I thought of family and friends back home, and my loneliness intensified. It occurred to me that the calm of the sea and lack of movement was the reason for this.

I turned and looked aft. It was the same. No waves, no horizon—nothing. I stared out into the haze for a long time. I prepared to lie down by the mast and read when a dolphin sprang from the water aft of the boat, smiled at me, and dove back. I raced to the railing to see where she had gone. I was exultant; there she was gliding gracefully near the surface, ogling at me.

She had stayed behind when the others had left. She had endured the misery of the storm rather than desert me. I had to get her some food so I dashed below, grabbed the

CHAPTER 9

box of butter cookies, and ran back up. As I tossed the cookies at my sea companion, my mood lightened; I was getting rid of some junk food, which was putting hated calories into my body. I actually chuckled at my next little triumph: the dolphin had responded by darting closer to the boat and leaping to catch my meager offerings.

The dolphin stayed with *Bravura* for two days and nights—four watches for me that were pure pleasure. My moods during these times were so much better than at any other time aboard the vessel that I began to ascribe events in a cause-and-effect manner because of her. She was responsible for moderate winds that had me beam, reaching right on the rhumb line. She was the reason for the extraordinarily beautiful sunsets. She had removed my omnipresent feelings of anxiety and depression.

I wandered on to thoughts of Coleridge's albatross and wondered if I had come under the spell of deep superstitions that sailors of yore had always had. In my classroom discussions, I had made a habit of pooh-poohing these slavish superstitions, but here I was at sea with my dolphin conjuring all sorts of things about her. Back in my bunk between watches, I dreamt about her and pondered the uncanny playfulness and wild freedom she had. I half-wished that I could dive into the water and join her for a romp. I recalled Balzac's Provencal soldier and his panther in the desert and was startled to discover that I thought of my dolphin in the same way.

After two days she left me. I didn't see her go. It might have been during my watches, but I kept telling myself that she went away when I was below. She had become a special romantic companion and, when she was gone, I felt like a jilted lover.

10

The day after I lost my dolphin, my mood steadily blackened and so did the Mediterranean. On my morning watch, the wind shifted three times in four hours and I had all I could do to tack abruptly and keep *Bravura* moving forward. I kept cursing and had conversations with Proteus and Triton, during which I chewed them out for all my trouble.

At the end of the watch, I checked my distance traveled and saw that I had gained a miserable two miles on the straight course of the rhumb line. I had probably tacked twenty miles or more back and forth but had nothing to show for it. "It's all your fault!" I shouted to the gods of the sea. "You're really screwing me today." As I hurled my last epithet, I turned and practically knocked down Roger.

He didn't ask me who the hell I was yelling at. He just took the wheel and stared ahead.

Dammit. He's not even going to give me a chance to explain. For all he knew, his jackass hired hand from New York has finally popped his cork.

Frustrated, I went below.

My twisted sleep filled with garish visions, but when I woke up, I smelt new air in the cabin. The sun's rays were intense, which quickly elevated my mood, as always. I grabbed a piece of moldy biscuit and went up to relieve Dick.

The sea was dead calm, and the temperature had risen. It was beautiful, and I found myself scanning the smooth water, hoping that my dolphin might be nearby. The sun's warmth brought good Karma, and the watch started off nicely. The sea, in its stillness, was like a painting. There wasn't even the slightest zephyr. I marveled that the knot meter was actually reading 0.00 and, even after an hour had elapsed, it hadn't budged.

Although the sun and warmth were welcome cohorts on my watch, after the second hour I began to fidget. The knot meter hadn't moved at all from its 0.00 reading and, although I couldn't detect the slightest stir in the air, I started to think it might be broken. I tapped it impulsively a couple of times, knowing before I did so that it wouldn't move.

I kept staring at the incredibly calm water and focusing my eyes on the horizon. Nothing. Not a ship, not a jumping fish, and, sadly, not a dolphin.

My mind wandered to stories I had read about sailing in the doldrums. These calm waters in zones just north of the equator had trapped sailing vessels for weeks or even longer. I had read of sailors really losing it because they

CHAPTER 10

could do nothing but wait and wait for some break in the calm.

At the end of my watch, I silently turned the helm over to Roger. "No use even touching the wheel," he said. "This calm will be with us for quite awhile."

Before I went down into the cabin, I took one last look at the knot meter. It read 0.00.

The next day the knot meter still hadn't moved. Various cloud formations had drifted overhead and, on my night watch, I thought I saw a ship's light to port way in the distance. My fidgeting continued. My impatience with the knot meter grew steadily and, by the next day, I was in a crazy state. I had to restrain myself from smashing the knot meter.

I might have tempered my state somewhat if I had given in to my temptation to demand that Roger check the knot meter. But I continually fought this notion because I couldn't stand another one of his condescending responses. I kept silent, but my blood pressure rose.

On my evening watch the next day, I heard Dick address Roger with a strange new tone in his voice as they were eating down in the cabin. "I've been calculating during this stretch of calm," he was saying. "If we don't get moving pretty soon, we'll never make Malta by the deadline."

"Not a damn thing we can do about it," Roger said, "unless you want to take a chance and run the diesel."

I peered down into the cabin and tried to read my crewmates' faces. Dick tried to meet Roger's challenging stare but slowly turned away. "No way," he said. "That engine has had it. Unless we make it to Malta before International closes up shop, we're finished."

Tears welled up in my eyes. I wanted to scream at the sea gods and lash out at the sea. My spirit was really broken, and I silently wondered if I would become hysterical and break down in front of the crew.

I whimpered on and on into the night. Later, I looked at my watch and, and seeing that I had only ten minutes to go before Roger relieved me, made sure that I wiped away all the tears and smears from my face. As I ran my sleeve across my clogged nose, I smelled something. I was just about to identify the smell as something in the air when I heard a sail flap.

I looked out at the water and saw the small cat's paws of an oncoming breeze.

Inside a minute the breeze had freshened, and so had I. I straightened the wheel and watched the sails steadily fill with air. As the boat picked up speed, I looked at the knot meter. It was reading 3.7 and increasing. I managed a croaking laugh to kick away my dissipating hysteria.

Upon hearing Roger climbing the cockpit stairs into the cabin, I stood smartly at the wheel. Despite his orneriness, he couldn't help but grin. "Looks like you finally appeased the gods, Joe," he said.

"No problem at all," I said. "I just made one of my secret libations, and Aeolus promptly granted my wish." I unclipped my harness and strode cockily down into the cabin.

My euphoria following the appearance of wind disappeared shortly after I consulted with Dick about the remaining distance to Malta. After double- checking the charts and projecting a low average for each day's distance on the rhumb line, he threw his pencil on the nav table.

CHAPTER 10

"Well, I suppose we could make it in time," he said. "But we'd have to average a helluva lot better than what we've done in the past two weeks."

And he had good reason to be apprehensive. If *Bravura*'s engine couldn't be repaired at Malta, the entire voyage would come to a humiliating end.

My depression returned but halfway through the rest period before my next watch, I noticed that the breeze had stiffened and *Bravura* was humming through the waves.

Later, when I came up on deck to begin my next watch, I was elated to see the knot meter registering a steady 7.1. The skies were clear, the temperature was moderate, and Aeolus's new wind had driven away the humidity. After settling in at the helm, I accepted a plateful of some stew that the guys had prepared. They had made this unappetizing dish many times before, but on this night I wolfed it down. Maybe it was the new wind making it taste better.

The boat was flying along, and I was urging her on. I was hoping the wind would increase so that we could make up the time lost during our doldrum days.

By the time I finished my meal, darkness had set in and the stars began flashing their cryptic Morse. I settled in, arranging my flashlight, hooking up my tape player, and folding my charts. I opened my cruising guide to the pages where illustrations of commercial ship's light signals were listed. I did the latter on all of my night watches. The Mediterranean was one of the most traveled commercial waterways on the planet, and there could be a lot of traffic along our rhumb line even though we had only seen a couple of ships way off in the distance during the last couple of weeks.

I pressed the start button on my tape player and heard Miles Davis playing "On Green Dolphin Street." Although my sea companion had deserted me, I had ample recompense hearing Miles, Coltrane, Cannonball, and Bill Evans run through the magnificent changes composed by Bronislaw Kaper.

I checked the knot meter and was excited to see it registering 7.3. We were nearing our theoretical maximum hull speed, and I raised a bottle of warm Coca-Cola to make a libation to Aeolus.

As I scanned the horizon, I spotted two ships way off to starboard. I thought they were headed away but, after rechecking the light directions in the cruising guide, I saw that they were making steam toward me.

The various combinations of red, white, and green lights displayed by all commercial ships are easy enough to recognize when you see them in a book. But when the ship in question is far off and at an angle and visibility is low, sometimes you can get confused. Was she headed toward me or going away? If she's coming my way, how soon do I have to make a course correction?

Questions like these would arise occasionally on night watches, but I had never had any problems.

As I was pleasantly relaxing, I noticed another ship's lights way off my port beam. I recognized the pattern of reds and whites and realized that this ship was approaching my course. She was far away, however, and I had plenty of time to observe her. Actually, I thought a few seconds later, maybe not as much time as I usually had.

Because *Bravura* was going so fast I was now forced to sit up and really concentrate. Alert now, I looked to my stern

CHAPTER 10

and saw two ships making a course that would take them right up my ass!

"Jesus Christ! Is the whole fucking international merchant marine fleet trying to run me down?"

I looked again at the light formations on each of the five ships. Right when I had I affirmed the course of one or two and turned around to see the others, I had to turn around again to check on the first ones.

The gap was closing fast. "Dammit. I sure hope they can see my radar beacon," I said to myself. By now two of the ships were abeam far enough away so that I knew they would pass harmlessly. But as I breathed the proverbial sigh of relief, I looked astern and got an eyeful of lights from the ships that were catching up to me very quickly.

"Man, I'm doing better than seven knots, and these bastards are going so fast it's as if I'm standing still."

I made a quick decision. I turned the wheel hard to port; I had to give myself more room. Of course, I immediately lost speed and had to haul in hard on the genoa to compensate.

I had several tense moments as the ships continued to gain on me. Finally, but only because I had made a ninety-degree course change, I was successfully moving out of their way. *Whew!*

I cursed again and again. What had started off as an exhilarating evening had turned into yet another stress-filled crisis at sea.

I spent the next half hour steadying myself. After getting well out of the way of those monster ships, I had to get back on the rhumb line and adjust the sails accordingly. The wind hadn't let up at all. *Hallelujah!* But it was a bit unusual because it was after 9:00 p.m., and the afternoon westerlies almost always died down after sunset.

Because the wind was still blowing strong, I had the devil of a time sheeting out the genoa as I moved the boat back to the rhumb. Normally, with such a wind blowing, any helmsman on watch would have called for assistance. But, once again, I was determined to go it alone and prove to Roger that I was up to the task. I was sure that he was fast asleep below, so the only way he could know what had happened on my watch was to check the log.

I made sure to write my entry of the multiple ships episode in prose as understated as possible, lest he think I was trying to exaggerate the events. Actually, because of my playing the whole thing down, he would never really know about the stress I underwent. So, what was I really proving? And to whom?

I spent the rest of my watch reflecting on all of this. At the end of my watch I went below, with no answer to the psychological tussles I was having.

As I lay in my bunk I realized how sore my hands, arms, and back were from all the maneuvering above without any help. *I really am a total jackass.* Exhausted, I fell quickly asleep.

11

I awoke refreshed. Somehow, I felt physically and mentally energized. As I slipped into my deck clothes, I marveled at how I could wake up from a night of mental anguish, having no residue whatsoever of the struggle. It was as if my subconscious was being scrubbed clean by some magic detergent. To the present day, I cannot explain any of this.

After eating some dry cereal, I went up on deck and felt the wind. It had not diminished a knot and Roger could not hide the pleasure he felt. "Made almost thirty knots in my four hours," he told me. "Not bad, eh?"

Indeed, it was an achievement worth bragging about. Only once during the voyage had I recorded such speed—but that had been during a six Beaufort gale.

The weather was perfect again today. A brilliant sunrise was engineering itself for me, and the boat was still knifing its way through the moderate seas.

Exhilarated, I couldn't help but try to do some distance forecasting. After I'd settled in, I gathered the charts around me and plotted our distance to Malta. I allowed for some reductions in wind velocity and tacking course changes. I checked and rechecked my figures and became excited.

By God, we could still do it. We could still make it to Valletta and get our engine fixed. With any kind of a break, we would see the coast of Malta in two and a half days. *Now, only the devil can stop us.* I clenched *Bravura*'s helm and winched a half turn on the jib to eke out more speed.

The watch went brilliantly and, by the end, I had achieved an incredible thirty-two knots dead on the rhumb—a new record for the voyage. I was as high as a kite.

I was careful not to brag in my log entry:

RECORDED 32-KNOT DISTANCE DURING WATCH WITH NO DEVIATION ON THE RHUMB LINE. WIND SPEED AVERAGED 14 KNOTS WITH LITTLE GUSTING.

For the first time in what seemed like an eternity, I slept like an infant. Instead of reading myself to sleep, I just turned off my lamp and went right to sleep. When I woke up, I was amazed to see I had slept for almost seven hours. But the really important news was the sound of the wind. Instantly, I knew it hadn't let up at all, and the boat was still cruising along. How long could such a breeze hold up? The weather would have to change soon. After all, this was the Mediterranean. Quickly I tapped myself on the side of my head. I was damned if I was going to let negative thoughts pervade my mind. I wanted to enjoy this stretch and wallow in my exciting anticipation of an on-time arrival.

I ate a tasty dinner of beef stew, Gouda cheese spread, and some damp Ritz crackers washed down with a can of

CHAPTER 11

ginger ale. Dick had outdone himself with the stew. It was absolutely gourmet. The great luck we were having with the wind had aroused high spirits among the crew. We all seemed to move crisper, and even Roger had lost most of the lines on his frowning forehead.

"Should see the south coast of Malta by midday tomorrow," I heard him say to Dick after I had relieved him for my evening watch. He had gone down to the galley. I was miffed that he chose to share this terrific forecast only with Dick, but I stifled the feeling as I settled into my seat at the helm. I wasn't going to allow anything to spoil my last watch of the voyage.

At my back the sun was setting in the midst of fluffy cumulus clouds. It was going to be another spectacular evening show. *Boy, I'm sure going to miss my nightly sunset.* Somehow all of the disasters and crises of the last weeks had evaporated with my new euphoria. I found this both odd and inexplicable. I had sworn that I would never forget a second of my misfortunes and here I was, behaving as if they hadn't even occurred. Amazing.

The wind was as steady as ever as I checked the gauges and looked up the mast to ensure the mainsail was sheeted properly. *Bravura* was in as balanced a state as I had ever experienced. Seldom could a boat have such a steady and powerful wind and at the same time be sailing through a smooth, following sea.

As I gathered my usual equipment about me—my tape player, harness, flashlight, and charts—I was subdued by a strange, unfamiliar melancholy. This would be my last watch on *Bravura*'s Mideast voyage. During many of the previous watches I had endured terrible feelings of loneliness, depression, anxiety, and hopelessness. I often wished that I had never set out to sea, that I could be back home lazing in front of the TV and, most of all, that I could be surrounded by family, friends, and colleagues. Instead, my powerful, romantic urges had gotten me into this miserable, life-threatening voyage. I had often cursed bitterly at my fate.

On this final evening, I realized I didn't want the voyage to end. A part of me wanted to continue to sail on and on. Even the realization that I would no longer have to endure Roger's hostility or Dick's insensitivity failed to raise my spirits. The struggles, which had depressed me so often, I now started to miss.

Amazing! My romantic fancies were battling my landlubber practicality. I shook my head and smiled. I realized that this war would continue in one way or another far into my future.

I slapped myself on the side of my head and pushed away these thoughts.

My chart confirmed that daylight would at last reveal land. The Maltese coast was now less than forty miles ahead on the rhumb. I widened my gaze and stared at the vast Mediterranean.

We had logged over twelve hundred miles since leaving Port Said and that evil desert. To the south lay Libya's Gulf of Sirte. After President Reagan's retaliatory bomb strike on Gaddafi's base a few years back, Libya had become America's archenemy. The Gulf of Sirte was a hundred miles due south of my position, and I shuddered at the closeness.

To the southwest lay Tunisia and the ancient location of Carthage, where Aeneas had wooed Dido. To the northeast lay Sicily where the ancient Greeks had built colonies that

CHAPTER 11

rivaled Athens in culture and sophistication. Farther to the northeast lay Crete, where I had spent many summers lecturing about the wonders of Theseus and the Minotaur.

I had sailed through Homer's wine-dark sea in the manner of Odysseus. All this history and mythology had dazzled my romantic head. I reached for my tape player and decided on some jazz.

BANG! BANG! I looked toward the sound of an explosion right above my head.

With trembling hands I reached for my flashlight to see what had happened. As the light beam shone in the darkness, I saw lines, shackles, and gear falling indiscriminately onto the deck from the top of the mast with horrific noises. I was paralyzed as I stared at the mast reeling freely in the blackness.

"On deck! On deck! On deck!" I shouted. Roger and Dick were in the cockpit before my last cry.

Roger grabbed my flashlight and pointed it at the top of the weaving mast eighty feet above us. "What the fuck happened?" I asked them. My hands were clutching the wheel so tightly that my fingers cramped.

I was still trying to steer the boat but realized that we were suddenly going nowhere; the mainsail had collapsed onto the deck with the other gear and was falling into the sea, its weight carrying it overboard.

 Grab the sheets—anything or we'll lose the sail," Roger ordered. Dick joined in by pulling on the sail and forcing it back onto the boat. They threw a critical look in my direction. I knew I should help them, but I was reluctant to leave the wheel. A second later, I realized the boat wasn't going anywhere, and my steering was pointless.

I joined in the struggle to pull in the main and, after what seemed like an hour, we finally got her in. The deck resembled a junkyard with piles of debris everywhere.

Panting from the struggle with the mainsail, we stared at each other, speechless. After a few minutes, during which he continuously waved the flashlight around the boat and up the mast, Roger spoke. He was eerily calm. "Midships stays must've snapped at the top of the stick."

I looked at him but didn't comprehend.

"Yep," said Dick, "but we're lucky the fore and aft stays held, or else the stick would have flown overboard."

The consensus of my crewmates upset me for two reasons. First, I really didn't understand what they were saying and, second, I couldn't believe how collected they were saying it. Once again, I was baffled by my brilliant sailor companions.

Still, I couldn't stop shaking. Whatever had happened, one thing was sure. We were in deep trouble. I realized that if I'd been standing amidships when the sky had fallen down, I would have been killed under the weight of the gear.

"We'd better get some hawser up from below and get a pulley going, or we'll lose the stick for sure if the seas come up." As Roger spoke he went below. Dick followed, and I was alone.

I felt stupid and useless. Anger swept over me. "On my watch. On my watch…" I kept repeating the phrase. Why did it have to happen on my watch?

As the guys came back up carrying thick ropes, I grabbed the steering wheel again to look like I was being productive. They didn't say anything, but I knew they were thinking that

CHAPTER 11

I was again being an idiot because the boat was dead in the water.

I left the wheel and helped them lug the long, heavy rope out from below. As we struggled, we felt the wind strengthen and saw the billowing waves rise. "Looks like we're in for a squall," said Roger matter-of-factly. I couldn't stop shaking.

"We have to heave-to," said Roger.

Although I had a vague notion of this classic maneuver, I had never had to do it. The guys were quickly at the bow and began hauling in the jib and backing it to the wind. "Get that rudder in position to heave-to," he said from amidships.

I knew that the rudder had to be turned to weather but, for a second, I was disoriented and turned it in the opposite direction. As the boat broached to the waves and my crewmates wondered what exactly I was doing, I quickly realized my error and spun the wheel again.

Bravura turned into the waves and the backed jib and weather helm steadied her. In a moment we were officially "hove-to," and I sat down to try and stop my shaking.

Even though the vessel was somewhat stabilized and pointing into the wind, the mast was loosely veering from side to side, and its huge weight was making ominous sounds. The absence of the beam stays was putting terrific pressure on the mast base; I thought that at any second it would rip right out of the deck and fall into the sea.

As I pondered this possibility, Roger and Dick focused on untangling the thick hawser rope and affixing a large pulley to one end. Their work was uncannily deliberate in this improbable crisis. I took a deep breath and gripped the steering pedestal tightly with both hands.

As I sat there steadying my nerves—but certainly not contributing anything—I looked at the waves coming at us and realized that although the boat was fore 'n'aft stabilized, we were being blown steadily south. If the squall kept up, we would soon be in the Libyan gulf.

As I digested this latest notion of dread, I also spotted Dick and Roger making their way aft into the cockpit. They had uncoiled a lot of hawser and were dragging the pulley end of it aft. When they finally got into the cockpit, they fell down exhausted.

I wanted to help comfort them. "You guys want a drink or something to eat?" I asked.

But the look I got said something like this: "How can you think of food at a time like this?"

We all felt the huge spray from the sea intensify. The wind was increasing, and waves were splashing everywhere. I felt tears well up in my eyes and a tightening in my throat. I wanted to scream at the boiling sea but instead tightened my grip on the pedestal.

"Well, I guess I'll start rigging a bosun's chair to climb up the stick," said Dick. He was calm now. And Roger just nodded his head in agreement as he pulled on the lapels of his foul weather gear to prevent himself from getting even more soaked.

"Climb up the stick?" I asked.

The guys looked at me with their standard the-dummy's-asking-an-idiotic-question-again expression. Roger stirred in his seat and picked up the heavy pulley. "We have to get this heavy line up over the top of the mast so we can

CHAPTER 11

stabilize it." His voice competed with the loud whistling of the wind. "Someone's got to get the line to the top of the mast."

After Dick come up from the cabin with some wooden boards, he and Roger constructed a seat that resembled a short hammock. They wound heavy line around the contraption and knotted it together expertly. The effort certainly tired them, and when they finished they fell against the bulkhead.

"I guess I'll go up," said Dick after a few minutes.

"No," said Roger. "It's gonna have to be me because I'm lighter."

"Yeah, but we've got to get the pulleys coordinated and anchored to the deck, and I've never done that."

They went back and forth each time injecting new reasons why one or the other should make the climb. I followed the argument and after more exchanges, I jumped in with an offer. "What about me going up?"

They looked at me blankly, but I thought I detected the beginning of a smirk forming on Roger's face.

"Look," I said. "From what you've both been saying, it seems that the best chance to stabilize the stick is if you're both down on the deck fastening the rigging. I don't know the first thing about doing that, and it would take forever trying to teach me. But I can certainly climb and take that rope and pass it through the pulley."

My brief forensic had hit home. I could tell by their docile expressions that I had made my point.

As they fitted me into the bosun's chair, I began to assess the implications of my brave words. The pounding white water and the mast reeling in the blackness brought on a whole new fear. I squeezed my legs tight against the base of the mast and gripped the line of the bosun's chair tightly to stop my shaking. But it must have seemed that I had found new determination by making these movements because the guys were supportive. From Dick I got a "Way to go, Joe," and from Roger—"You've got a good set of balls."

This last comment galvanized my emotions, and with some new determination from deep within the romantic bowels of my consciousness, I grinned confidently down at the guys as they pulled at the ropes of my rig. I rose rapidly and, after taking a peek down from about thirty feet up and feeling a sliver of panic in my spine, turned my head quickly upward to the top of the reeling mast.

I had no sooner got there when the end of the hawser line was in my hand; I fitted it through the steel rung at the top of the stick. As I pulled more of the line through and down to the guys, I noticed the ragged edges of metal where the stays had ripped off.

I was so determined to get the ropes through the pulleys as the guys kept sending more gear up to me that, somehow, the fear from being eighty feet up on a mast on a crippled sailboat in the middle of a gale didn't paralyze me. There is absolutely no way that I can explain this.

Because of a combination of adrenaline, intense concentration, and sheer luck, I continued moving lines through the top of the mast for almost three hours. Steadily, the reeling of the mast became less and less, and toward the end of the work the stick became almost rigid. In a carefully executed plan, Roger and Dick winched various sections of the thick hawser that I had threaded down onto cleats and other fixtures on the deck.

CHAPTER 11

When it came time for me to descend on the bosun's chair, I did so carefully as the guys lowered me inch by inch. As I finally stood on the deck clutching the mast, both of my crewmates gave me a pat on the shoulder. It was the most triumphant feeling for me on the whole voyage.

By now the black night had passed and a gray, wet dawn loomed above. "When did it start to rain?" I asked.

Dick laughed. "It was raining when you started climbing hours ago."

I was amazed that I couldn't remember.

"Let's all try to get some rest," said Roger. "Later on we'll see if we can add more tension to our jury-rigged rope stays. Maybe we can even hoist a sail on her."

Exhausted, we all went below. The boat was still hove-to, and we were losing distance on our course as she was being pushed southward in the storm.

But all of that didn't matter. We had saved our mast and were still afloat and fortunate to have survived the night. Right now we needed rest, and we all promptly fell into our bunks totally spent.

12

I awoke hours later twisting wildly in my bunk. I was having multiple nightmares all something vaguely to do with drowning. I pushed these cobwebs out of my rising consciousness and sat up. I turned over and looked out the porthole. The white water was still beating against *Bravura*'s freeboard, and the wind was still howling.

I stood up and worked my way into the galley, grabbing at the bulkhead to steady myself. The boat was still being shunted to and fro from the storm. I wasn't hungry but pulled some crackers out of a bag lying near the stove. I was feeling weak and didn't know what fresh disaster awaited me when I climbed up top.

In the cockpit I saw Roger and Dick at the mast working the winches again. They were tightening the ropes. Some of them must have slackened during our rest.

I watched them intently. They were working steadily, calmly, efficiently. Once again, they were exhibiting the necessary trappings of seasoned sailors. Whatever their social shortcomings may have been, I realized that I certainly wouldn't be alive without their experience and determination.

"We can't do anything until this damn storm eases," said Roger. "We've lost over a hundred miles and we're getting close to the Libyan coastline...Might as well get as much rest as we can."

Oh my God, I thought. We nearly killed ourselves in the storm. Now what will happen if we run into those lunatic Libyans?

After awhile I staggered below, once again depressed, once again feeling hopeless against the incredible fates of this voyage.

I lay in my bunk all morning and into the early afternoon. The storm still raged and our southward drift continued unabated. Sometime after, I crawled into the galley while listening to my stomach cry out for food. I looked around and spotted an open peanut butter jar. I grabbed it and started knifing chunks of it onto a piece of black bread that lay beside the jar. How much peanut butter have I consumed on this voyage? I wondered as I bit into the crude sandwich. If it weren't for peanut butter, I decided, I probably would be skin and bones by now.

While I was munching in the galley, I suddenly became aware of new stability on the boat. I peered out a porthole. Sure enough, no white water.

I put away the jar, washed off the knife, and then scrambled up the cockpit stairway, still chewing the food. Not only had the seas ebbed but, as I turned to the west, a bolt of sunshine hit me in the eyes. The sun was sneaking out

CHAPTER 12

from behind a lingering, heavy cloud layer; the miserable storm was now moving rapidly eastward.

"Thank you, Poseidon!" I shouted, holding my peanut butter sandwich high, pretending that it was a wine glass and I was making a libation to the sea gods.

I cupped my hands around my mouth so as to hail my crewmates and welcome them to the blissful change. But I hesitated and then dropped my hands. I decided not to share this exhilaration. I wanted to be alone and reflect on what had happened. I thought about the madness of the storm and the terrible crisis we had undergone with the breaking of the stays. I tried to focus on the intense fears I had had and figure out things.

Somehow I couldn't retrieve those dark moments. Somehow the terror of the last days wasn't as terrible anymore. Once again I was failing in my efforts to understand my consciousness. I smirked as the lyrics of a notable pop tune came into my head…"What's it all about, Alfie?"

After awhile, Roger came up on deck carrying two cups of coffee. He handed me one without saying anything. I took it from him and together we stared at the bow and the horizon to the north. It seemed some new bond had formed between us.

Roger turned his scrutinizing sailor's eye to the top of the mast. "Well, she seems to be holding firm. We won't have to tighten the ropes anymore." He put down his coffee mug and rubbed his hands together. "I'll go down and rouse Dick out of his bunk. Then we can try to jury rig a sail to the mast and maybe get going again."

I watched the hopeful expression on his face and took a sip of coffee. He turned to me and started to say something else, but he looked past me and his forehead tightened.

"Uh oh," he said. "Looks like we're going to have company." I spun around to look aft and saw a large gray vessel motoring behind us and moving fast in the water.

"Doesn't look like a commercial boat," I said turning to Roger. He was already taking binoculars out of the case from the pedestal shelf. He held them to his eyes and focused.

It didn't take him more than a couple of seconds to identify the boat. He put the binoculars down and rubbed his eyes. "It's a gunboat," he said. "And she's flying the Libyan flag."

I started to reach for the binoculars but realized that I didn't need them because the boat had gained so much on us in just a few moments. All we could do was stand idly as the sleek gleaming hull moved toward us. She was pushing a lot of water in front of her, and as she moved she veered to port; when she was abeam of us she cut her engines. The bow wave that she carried came toward us and, as I stared at a row of black-uniforms on the deck, overtook us and made *Bravura* heel ominously from side to side.

As the gray monster moved closer to us and filled the horizon, I gazed at the huge green flag flying from the stern. It was the only single-color flag in the world. It was unmistakable. I had read that it was a symbol of Islam and the Libyan people.

One of the uniforms on the ship's starboard beam pulled out a huge bullhorn and barked out something unintelligible but incredibly loud. I didn't think any bullhorn could amplify sound so intensely.

CHAPTER 12

We didn't have to figure out what he said because as he spoke a detail of the black uniforms had moved a large zodiac from the deck into the water. By the time the amplified speech had ended, the detail of armed military made their raft fast to our port lifelines.

The soldiers filed out of the raft and moved across our decks brandishing automatic weapons. A few of them stared at the American flag we were flying.

I stood limply next to Roger as the bodies moved swiftly all over *Bravura* and suddenly noticed Dick next to me. There we were, like three mice waiting for a huge cat to pounce on us.

We had come all this way, endured all of the countless challenges, and survived all of the misery only to be swallowed up by our worst possible adversary within a day's sail of our destination and safety.

Tears welled up once again in my eyes at the hopelessness.

After completing a quick search of the boat, the invaders stood at attention as their leader emerged from the cabin and mounted the deck, staring down at us. He was tall for an Arab, with a dark face buried behind a swarthy beard and black aviation glasses.

He looked us up and down scornfully. "You are trespassing in the official waters of Libya." His articulate English startled me. "What is the purpose of your intrusion?"

Roger looked up at him rubbing his eyes and face. "We are a pleasure boat circumnavigating the globe. Our engine is broken, and we also broke our mast in a storm. We are making for Malta to seek repairs to our boat." He looked down after speaking. He had given this speech to officials countless times in the past months, but this time his words held a hint of resignation. We were finished; he knew his explanation was a waste of time.

The Libyan officer stared at us for a long moment and then turned and shouted orders to his men. Then he waved at the gunboat in the distance as his cadre brought long ropes out of the zodiac.

When he turned back to us, he said, "Go below and stay in your cabins." His men were pointing their guns at us. We filed below like little children.

I lay in my bunk and half-listened to the noises. It was easy to figure out what was happening. The Libyans had tied the ropes to our bow cleats and had gone back to the mother ship leaving what seemed to be only a couple of their group in our cockpit. Quickly, the roar of their huge diesels could be heard, and we were off being towed.

I pushed the waves and waves of black thoughts from my mind. We would be imprisoned of course. We would become hostages and tortured like so many Americans had been by terrorists in the past decade. We would never see our families again, would die a miserable death in some godforsaken corner of this horrific desert nation.

I kept fighting my thoughts but somehow must have fallen into a fitful sleep. I awoke much later and saw that it was night. We were still under tow and moving incredibly fast through the water. I couldn't believe that the tow ropes could hold, pulling our heavy sailboat that quickly. I didn't understand why it was taking so long to get to the Libyan coastline based on our last position when the storm ended.

I tossed all of my thoughts and observations aside and wanted to force tears into my eyes. They wouldn't come, so I just sat at the end of my bunk in a trance. After awhile, I

CHAPTER 12

thought of trying to sneak out and go into either Roger's or Dick's cabin. I decided against it, thinking that if I was caught I would be shot or something.

I lay back down and slept some more. The next time I awoke, daylight was streaming in, and the towing had slowed down. We were in a harbor somewhere because I heard the sound of other boats and distant voices.

Someone knocked at my cabin door, and when I opened it one of the black uniforms bowed and motioned me out.

Dick and Roger were already in the cockpit. We were, indeed, in a busy harbor, and the black uniforms were removing our towlines from the gunboat. We were at a long concrete dock, and the soldiers were affixing dock lines from metal bollards on the shore to our bow and stern.

Just then a civilian came out of our cabin with oil all over his hands. He had evidently been in our engine room. "Good day, gentlemen," he said politely. "I would shake your hands, but I'm full of diesel oil." He put his hands out and we saw what he meant.

"Who…er…who are you?" Roger asked with trepidation.

"I am Lorca Vandraga," said the smiling face. "I am senior mechanic for International Diesel here in Valletta."

www.ingramcontent.com/pod-product-compliance
Lightning Source LLC
Chambersburg PA
CBHW020005050426
42450CB00005B/322